Advanced
Fingerstyle Guitar

**This easy-to-understand guide to advanced and professional level
fingerpicking features 33 highly playable tunes arranged or composed by
leading guitarists, in both clear tablature and standard notation.
By Ken Perlman**

D1616277

~ Acknowledgments ~
Cover photo by David Bagnall
Thanks to Holly Staver for her invaluable help in
preparation of this manuscript.
~
Thanks to two New York City music stores: Matt Umanov Guitars and
The Music Inn for assistance in album research.
~
Thanks to Rick Cyge of Wood & Strings Music Center (Arlington, MA)
for helping me proofread the music and tablature.
~
Thanks to the many musicians and music lovers I've encountered
in my travels for their encouragement and friendship.

ISBN 1-57424-124-9
SAN 683-8022

Author's Bio

Ken Perlman has been active internationally since the mid-1970s as a prominent teacher of fingerstyle guitar. He has served on guitar faculties at prestigious music-teaching festivals around the world, he is guitar columnist for *Sing Out!* magazine, and he has written frequently on guitar instruction for *Acoustic Guitar, Acoustic Musician* and several other periodicals. He has written two other guitar books *Fingerstyle Guitar* and *Fingerpicking Fiddle Tunes* (both published by Centerstream) and he has also recorded a video companion for *Fingerstyle Guitar*.

Ken's solo recordings include *Northern Banjo* (Copper Creek), *Island Boy* (Wizmak), *Devil in the Kitchen* (Marimac), *Live in the U.K.* (Halshaw) and *Clawhammer Banjo* and *Fingerstyle Guitar Solos* (Folkways).

Ken is also widely known as a master of clawhammer-style banjo. His banjo books are *Clawhammer Style Banjo* (Centerstream), *Melodic Clawhammer Banjo* (Music Sales), *Everything You Wanted to Know about* Clawhammer Banjo (Mel Bay) and *Basic Clawhammer Banjo* (Mel Bay). He has been a regular columnist for *Banjo Newsletter* for nearly two decades and he has served as music-director for two banjo-teaching festivals: the Maryland Banjo Academy and Banjo Camp North.

For over a decade, Ken has been actively engaged in a project studying the music and customs of traditional fiddlers on Prince Edward Island in Eastern Canada. He has produced several works on the subject, including a tune book called *The Fiddle Music of Prince Edward Island: Celtic and Acadian Tunes in Living Tradition* (Mel Bay) and a two-CD anthology entitled *The Prince Edward Island Style of Fiddling* (Rounder Records).

He lives and works in the Boston area.

CD Playlist
All tunes played by Ken Perlman unless otherwise indicated

1. Georgia Camp Meeting	0:34	22. Taylor's Twist	1:07
2. Travelin' Man	1:03	23. Bonnie Charlie	0:57
3. Living in the Country	0:46	24. Billy in the Lowground	1:06
4. Brown's Ferry Blues	0:40	25. O'Carolan's Welcome	0:54
5. Sunday Street	1:19	26. Tracy's Rag	2:13
6. Blue Railroad Train	0:41	27. Le Voyage Pour L'lrlande	1:08
7. Piano Mover's Rag	0:47	28. Hot Chestnuts	3:15
8. Careless Love	0:41	played by Glenn Jenks:	
9. Police Dog Blues	0:57	from the LP, *Antidote*.	
10. Bullfrogs on Your Mind	0:31	29. Andy's Augmented Rag	0:55
played by Geoff Bartley: from the		played by Andy Polon:	
CD, *Blues Beneath the Surface*.		from the CD,	
11. Silver City Bound	1:22	*New York on Six Strings a Day*.	
12. Big Road Blues	0:36	30. The Way You Look in the Dark	2:04
13. Hesitation Blues	1:06	31. Paragon Rag	2:46
14. Trouble in Mind	1:00	32. Mary-Joan,	
15. Cold Feet Blues	1:11	or the Siege of Leningrad	2:21
16. The Mississippi Blues	1:16	played by Erik Frandsen, live at	
17. Tobin's Favourite	0:31	The Bottom Line in New York City.	
18. Curranta for Mrs		33. Philosophy Rag	4:09
Elizabeth Murcott	0:53	played by Nick Katzman:	
19. Banish Misfortune	1:05	from the LP,	
20. Foxhunter's Jig	0:32	*Sparkling Ragtime & Hardbitten Blues*.	
21. Swingin' on a Gate	0:55		

~ Notes on the Accompanying CD~

- Ken Perlman's renditions were recorded, edited and mixed at Wellspring Sound in Acton, Mass. by sound engineer Eric Kilburn. The entire recording was also mastered at Wellspring.

- To ensure that this book's entire repertoire would fit on a single CD, many repeats and reprises called for in the notation were omitted from recorded versions.

- Cut #32 (Mary Joan...) was transferred from a cassette in the possession of Erik Frandsen. Despite its poor fidelity, it nevertheless represents the only decent recording of him playing this piece (Frandsen has not been playing much fingerstyle guitar of late, and felt he wasn't in a position to re-record). The reader should be aware that the guitar had to be run at a fairly low sound-level in order to keep tape hiss down to an acceptable level. You'll probably want to turn the volume up to get the flavor of this cut. In the interests of eardrum preservation, however, please remember to turn the volume down again at the start of cut #33!

Contents

Chapter-opening photos:
top, Lynn Clayton (photo by Kevin Johnson)
bottom, Nick Katzman

(NOTE: All tunes arranged by Ken Perlman unless otherwise indicated).

1

Introduction

Introduction to the New Edition

To paraphrase one highly successful late-20th century ad campaign, *Advanced Fingerstyle Guitar* is really two books in one. To the already advanced player, it's an excellent tune book that features 33 interesting and highly playable guitar arrangements. To the ambitious intermediate player, it serves as a clear and detailed guide to the technical expertise and theoretical knowledge required to bridge the gap to the advanced level.

Advanced Fingerstyle was written as both supplement and sequel to my *Fingerstyle Guitar* book (also published by Centerstream). *Fingerstyle Guitar* covered most basic fingerpicking techniques. Because the field is so large and varied, however, I had to move along at a pretty fast clip, and just touch on – or ignore entirely – a number of techniques and specialties that would have made interesting side trips. What's more, to facilitate learning I concentrated on a basic form of fingerstyle made up largely of two parts: melody and bass line.

Advanced Fingerstyle brings into clear focus many subtleties, technical nuances and playing styles that *Fingerstyle Guitar* unavoidably glossed over. What's more, *Advanced Fingerstyle* breaks quite a bit of new ground. It explores a number of new rhythmic devices and techniques, it offers a more varied and challenging role to the plucking-hand thumb, and it introduces a fuller-sounding approach to the guitar that includes important musical events *between* the melody and bass lines. Among the new techniques and stylistic devices covered are the drone bass, the walking bass, the boogie-woogie bass, the stride bass, the stride-drone bass, slapping the strings, sixteenth notes, harmonics, the Scotch snap, the vibrato choke, Baroque tuning, Dad-gad tuning, "partial" barre-chords and movable jazz-chord forms.

Advanced Fingerstyle also explores those aspects of harmony useful to fingerpickers, such as thirds, sixths, tenths, triads, seventh chords, augmented and diminished chords, compound chords, altered chords, chord voicings, voice leading, the circle of fifths, modulation, modal harmony and harmony determination. Each subject receives a detailed capsule treatment in terms easy for a guitarist to understand. While these treatments are not intended as a substitute for a serious study of harmony, they will help you better understand what you are playing and assist you in ultimately creating your own arrangements and compositions.

In order to help you apply all this knowledge, chord indications appear above the standard notation staff. This lets you keep track of the background harmony as you play through even the most complex up-the-neck pieces.

The Tunes

There's been such a wealth of interesting and challenging material composed or arranged for fingerstyle guitar in the last couple of decades, that compiling the 33 pieces included in this collection was a real pleasure. I was able to select tunes – not only because of their ability to clearly illustrate technical concepts – but because they were musically intriguing or just plain fun to play! In this collection, then, you'll find challenging breaks or variations for a number of tunes and several lengthy pieces that offer you a wide range of expression and a real chance to grow as a musician.

The tunes in *Advanced Fingerstyle* are organized according to genre. Chapter 4, "Alternating Bass Pieces," adds some new dimensions to this popular fingerpicking style. Chapter 5, "The Country Blues," centers on the style originally popularized by such legendary guitarists as Rev. Gary Davis, Blind Blake, Lightnin' Hopkins, Willie Brown, Son House and Robert Johnson. It introduces a number of specialized techniques, and offers a new, more effective method for notating and thinking about the style's complex rhythms. Chapter 6, "Melodic Guitar: Fiddle Tunes and Related Forms," includes a number of new fiddle tune arrangements along with some helpful discussions and exercises designed to help you master this idiom. Chapter 7, "From Ragtime to Riches: The Frontiers of Fingerstyle" explores the fields of ragtime and chord-melody guitar, offering a number of groundbreaking fingerstyle compositions by some of today's most innovative players.

How to Use this Book

As the title implies, *Advanced Fingerstyle* is not a book for beginners. In fact, I strongly recommend that you make your way through the first six or seven chapters of *Fingerstyle Guitar* (or the equivalent material in some comparable course of study) before tackling this book

The tunes in *Advanced Fingerstyle* are presented more or less in order of difficulty, but they are not closely graded. You can either tackle them systematically, or just skip around and try your hand at those pieces that appeal most to you. If you elect to skip around, be aware that you can locate explanations for any unfamiliar notations or techniques by referring to the index, Chapter 2 ("Tablature and Standard Guitar Notation") or Chapter 3 ("Fingerstyle Techniques").

Important new techniques in *Advanced Fingerstyle* appear under major headings. They are then illustrated by musical examples or exercises, and used immediately in one or more pieces. Specific applications of new techniques or playing principles are dealt with in the *Technique* sections that follow many of the tunes in the book.

If you learned to fingerpick from *Fingerstyle Guitar*, you may well have bogged down trying to make the transition from basic alternating bass style (illustrated in the first seven chapters) to fiddle tunes and ragtime (chapters 8-11). If so, you will find the tunes in Chapters 4 and 5 of *Advanced Fingerstyle* an excellent intermediate stage to help you make this transition more smoothly.

A New Life for Advanced Fingerstyle

Fingerstyle Guitar was probably the first book to attempt a serious step-by-step analysis of fingerpicking. The idea was simple: starting from scratch, new techniques were introduced gradually, and each tune was only slightly more difficult than its immediate predecessor. Since at the time this was a radically new approach to the subject, I had no idea how it would be accepted. I was very pleased by the outcome. The book was highly praised by the major acoustic music periodicals, thousands of copies were sold to individuals and libraries around the world and the work was even translated into German (German title: *Fingerpicking perfekt*). Even more gratifying, Fingerstyle *Guitar* has become a classic in the field of guitar pedagogy, and on my performing tours I am constantly encountering guitarists who have used the book to learn their basic skills.

Advanced Fingerstyle, on the other hand, has throughout most of its existence been a book in search of an identity. Just as it first went to press (under the title *More Fingerstyle Guitar*) the publisher got caught up in a merger and immediately dismantled its music-books division. As a result *More Fingerstyle* was published but never actually distributed, and it was only reviewed by a few periodicals. Centerstream then took the book on and published it with a new title, namely *Contemporary Fingerstyle Guitar*. At first this title seemed to do the trick, but after a few years we began to suspect that the term "contemporary" was becoming increasingly less descriptive. If nothing else, a new generation of guitarists wasn't nearly as familiar with the artists, genres and individual pieces represented in the book as guitarists in general had been when the work was first published. Clearly some changes were called for!

In the end we decided on two alterations for the new edition. First, we changed the title to *Advanced Fingerstyle Guitar*, which more accurately reflects what this book is all about. Second, we put together a companion CD to illustrate all the great tunes in this volume. Hopefully, this will help introduce this repertoire to a new generation of players.

When I first put together this volume, I invited a number of prominent fingerpickers to contribute a tune from their performing repertoire. Photographs of these artists appear throughout the book, and a capsule biography of each artist appears alongside his or her tune.

When the idea of putting together a companion CD for this new edition first came up, I wanted each guest picker to illustrate his or her own tune. Unfortunately, enough time had elapsed since the first edition was published to make this plan impractical. We were able to arrange for a few performances by guest pickers, however, and I trust that you will enjoy them.

In alphabetical order, these guest pickers are:

Geoff Bartley (Massachusetts)
Pierre Bensusan (France)
Rory Block (New York State)
Gill Burns (England)
Lynn Clayton (England)
Erik Frandsen (New York City)
Wendy Grossman (now living in England)
Glenn Jenks (Maine)
Pete Kairo (Massachusetts)
Nick Katzman (now living in Germany)
Colin Linden (Ontario, Canada)
Woody Mann (New York City)
Andy Polon (New York City)
Pete Seeger (New York State)
Janet Smith (California)
Michael Soloway (New York City)
Happy Traum (New York State)
Dave Van Ronk (New York City)

Good Pickin'!
Ken Perlman,
Arlington, Massachusetts

2
Tablature
and Standard
Guitar Notation

Chapter-opening photos:
top, Erik Frandsen (photo by Irene Young);
bottom, Michael Soloway (photo by Lois Dreyer)

In this chapter, I'll review the tablature system introduced in *Fingerstyle Guitar*, along with those aspects of standard music notation that apply specifically to guitar. The notation for a certain few techniques is somewhat different in this book from that employed in the first book, and special note will be made of any such changes.

The Staff

The tablature used here is written on a staff of six lines (see figure 2–1). Each line stands for a string on the guitar. The highest line represents the first (high E) string, the lowest represents the sixth (low E) string, and so on. Numbers on the lines represent frets—1 stands for first fret, 2 for second fret, and so on (see figure 2–2). A zero on any line means that the corresponding string is to be played "open" (unfretted). Notes to be played simultaneously are aligned vertically, as shown in figure 2–3.

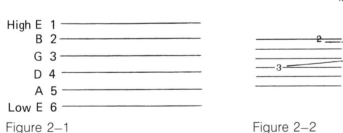

Figure 2–1

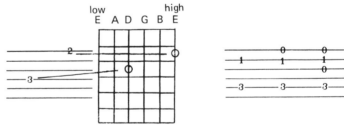

Figure 2–2

Figure 2–3

In the first book, the tablature and standard notation versions of each tune were presented separately. In this book, both appear on adjoining staffs, as shown in figure 2–4.

Figure 2–4

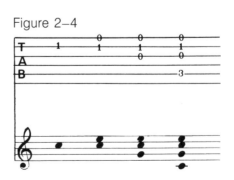

Meter

Musical time is measured in beats. Beats are organized into units called measures, divided from each other on the staff by vertical measure lines (see figure 2–5). In most tunes, each measure contains the same number of beats. The note falling on the first beat (the *downbeat*) of each measure is always *accented* (emphasized).

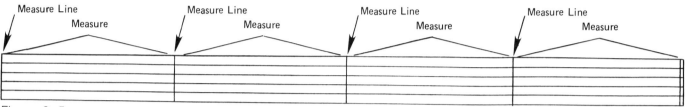

Figure 2–5

PICKUP NOTES

Any notes occurring before the first accented beat of a tune are called *pickup notes* (or *upbeat* notes) and are set off to the left of the first measure line, as shown in figure 2–6.

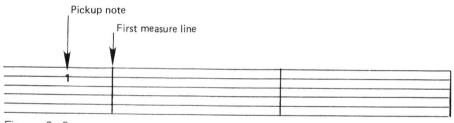

Figure 2–6

TIME SIGNATURES

Time signatures are placed at the beginning of each piece and offer two kinds of information. The top number tells how many beats are contained within each measure, while the bottom number tells what kind of note (half, quarter, eighth, and so on) is counted as one beat. Figure 2–7 briefly explains the time signatures found in this book. For more detailed information on the various time signatures, consult the index and/or the original *Fingerstyle Guitar*.

Figure 2–7

TIME SIGNATURE	NUMBER BEATS PER MEASURE	KIND OF NOTE COUNTED AS ONE BEAT
$\frac{2}{2}$ (¢)	2	Half note
$\frac{4}{4}$	4	Quarter note

Figure 2–7 (*continued*)

TIME SIGNATURE	NUMBER BEATS PER MEASURE	KIND OF NOTE COUNTED AS ONE BEAT
3 4	3	Quarter note
2 4	2	Quarter note
6 8	6	Eighth note
9 8	9	Eighth note
12 8	12	Eighth note

Rhythm Notation

Rhythm notation tells the player how long each note is to sound. The rhythm notation used with this tablature system is virtually identical to the one used for standard music notation, in which different stem shapes are used to show time value (see figure 2–8). Observe that the particular numbers appearing in the tab notation column are just examples. Any number can, of course, appear along with any stem shape.

Figure 2–8

TAB NOTATION	STANDARD NOTATION	KIND OF NOTE	NOTE VALUE IN ¼ TIME
		Quarter note	1 beat
		Eighth note	½ beat
		Multiple eighth notes	½ beat each
		Triplet	3 notes, ⅓ beat each
		Dotted quarter	1½ beats
		Sixteenth notes	¼ beat each
		"Dotted pair" dotted eighth note plus sixteenth note	¾ beat + ¼ beat
		Grace note, double grace note	Virtually no time value (very quick notes)

WHOLE AND HALF NOTES

Whole and half notes are notated in this tablature system by placing a box around a tablature entry or column of entries. A half note has an added stem, while a whole note has none, as shown in figure 2–9.

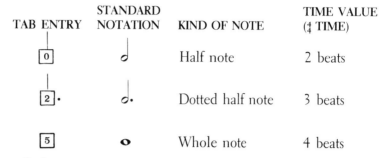

TAB ENTRY	STANDARD NOTATION	KIND OF NOTE	TIME VALUE (¼ TIME)
0	♩	Half note	2 beats
2 ·	♩·	Dotted half note	3 beats
5	𝅝	Whole note	4 beats

Figure 2–9

RESTS

Rest symbols are employed to tell you when not to play. They are exactly the same for both tablature and standard notation (figure 2–10).

SYMBOL	NAME	DON'T PLAY FOR
▬	Whole rest	4 beats
▬	Half rest	2 beats
𝄽	Quarter rest	1 beat
𝄽·	Dotted quarter rest	1½ beats
𝄾	Eighth rest	½ beat

Figure 2–10

TIED NOTES

⌢ or ⌣

Figure 2–11

When a tie (figure 2–11) connects two identical notes on the same string, the second note is *not* plucked. Instead, the first note is permitted to sound for its own time value *plus the duration of the second note,* as shown in figure 2–12.

Figure 2–12

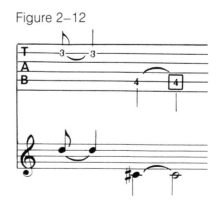

TIED NOTES AND SYNCOPATION

Throughout most of *Fingerstyle Guitar*, a very visual approach to notating syncopations was employed in which a syncopated note was often followed by a rest, as shown in figure 2–13a. A more precise notation, shown in figure 2–13b, uses tied notes to show the exact duration of the syncopated note. This more precise system was introduced near the end of *Fingerstyle Guitar* and is used exclusively in this book. A review of syncopation appears in Chapter 3.

Figure 2–13a

Figure 2–13b

The Plucking Hand

The following symbols will occasionally be employed in both the tablature and standard notation staffs to indicate plucking-hand finger use:

> i - index finger
>
> m - middle finger
>
> r - ring finger

THUMB VERSUS FINGERS

For both tablature and standard notation, the stem for notes played by the thumb (thumb notes) originates *below* the staff, while the stem for notes played by the fingers (finger notes) originates *above* the staff, as shown in figure 2–14. Observe that notes and rests in the fingers

Figure 2–14

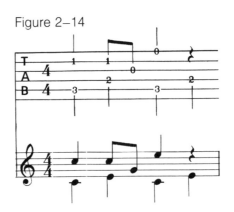

portion of the staff are counted separately from notes and rests in the thumb portion of the staff. Both portions of the staff must add up to a full complement of beats.

SHARING THE MELODY BETWEEN THUMB AND FINGERS

When the melody of a tune is split up between the thumb and the fingers, the double-stem notation shown in figure 2–15 often appears in *both* tablature and standard notation. Any note with a stem originating below the staff is played by the thumb, *even if it also has a stem originating above the staff.* The top stem of a double-stem note merely shows the continuity of the melody line.

Figure 2–15

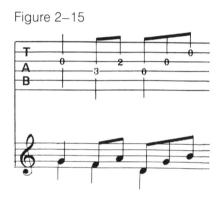

SIMULTANEOUS NOTES

In tablature, when two or more finger notes are played simultaneously, only the topmost has an attached stem. In standard notation, a single stem connects all finger notes, as shown in figure 2–16a. In both tablature and standard notation, when the lowest note in a simultaneous group is played by the thumb, that note has an attached stem originating below the staff, as shown in figure 2–16b. Observe that the brackets employed in the first book to separate finger notes from thumb notes are no longer in use.

Figure 2–16a

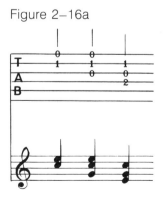

Figure 2–16b

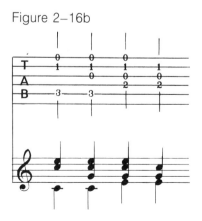

The following symbols are used to denote fretting-hand fingers. These symbols appear routinely in chord diagrams, fingering diagrams, and *standard notation* staffs to suggest efficient finger use. Observe that the symbol "T" also appears in *tablature* staffs to show instances of thumb fretting.

T = thumb

1 = first or index finger

2 = second or middle finger

3 = third or ring finger

4 = fourth or little finger

POSITION NOTATION (I, II, III, V . . .)

Position notation is a good way of indicating optimal fretting-hand location. Position is notated by placing Roman numerals above the *tablature* staff. In first position (symbol: I), the first finger *stops* (presses down) notes on the first fret of any string, the second finger stops notes on the second fret of any string, the third finger stops notes on the third fret of any string, and the fourth finger stops notes on the fourth fret of any string.

In second position (II), the fretting hand is located higher on the neck and the first finger stops notes on the second fret, the second finger stops notes on the third fret, the third finger stops notes on the fourth fret, and the fourth finger stops notes on the fifth fret. In fifth position (V), the first finger stops notes on the fifth fret, the second finger stops notes on the sixth fret, and so on. In seventh position (VII), the first finger stops notes on the seventh fret; in tenth position (X), the first finger stops notes on the tenth fret, and so on.

BARRES AND HALF BARRES

In a full barre, all six strings of the guitar are pressed down at a particular fret by the flat underside of the first finger. In a half barre, two to four strings, depending on context, are pressed down by the underside of the first finger. These are indicated above the *tablature* staff by placing a Roman numeral (to signify a fret) next to a "barre" or "½ barre" notation. So "barre II" indicates a full barre at the second fret, "barre V" indicates a full barre at the fifth fret, "½ barre VII" indicates a half barre at the seventh fret, and so on.

CHORD SYMBOLS

The chord symbols appearing above the *tablature* staff indicate that a particular passage is best played while the fretting hand is pressing

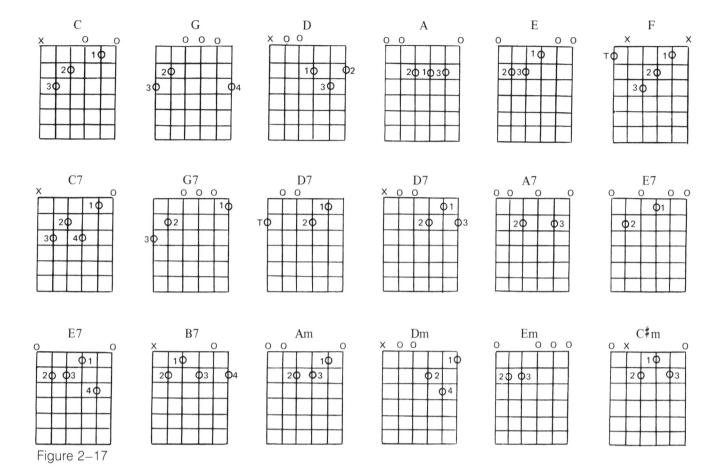

Figure 2–17

down one of the basic chord forms shown in figure 2–17 or introduced later. Chord symbols above the standard notation staff refer to the *harmony* of a passage, rather than to a particular chord form (see Chapter 4).

CHORD FORMS MOVED UP THE NECK

Any basic chord form can be moved up the neck and combined with open strings. This is notated above the *tablature* staff by indicating the chord plus a Roman numeral for the fret to which it is moved. So "C7-III" indicates a C7 chord moved up to the third fret, "D-VII" indicates a D chord moved up to the seventh fret, and so on. Forms that are often moved up the neck in this manner are known as *movable chords*.

BARRE CHORDS

Barre chords are basic chord forms played under a full barre, as shown in figure 2–18. These are notated above the tablature staff by showing the barre chord, plus a Roman numeral for the fret at which it is to be pressed down. So "Barre E-V" indicates that a barre E chord is played at the fifth fret, "Barre A7-III" means that a barre A7 chord is played at the third fret, and so on.

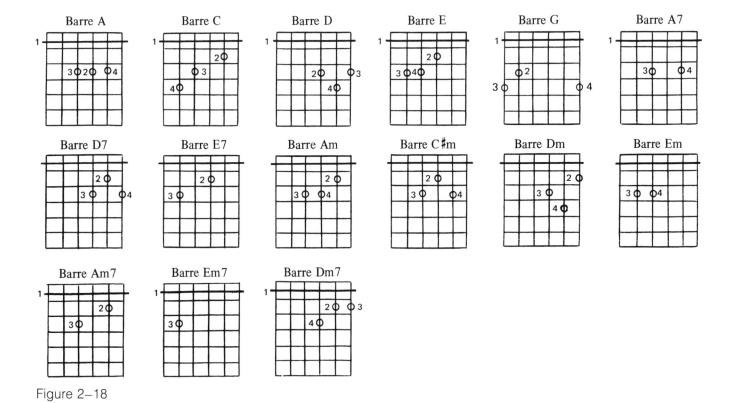

Figure 2–18

SPECIAL FINGERING DIAGRAMS

When a series of notes requires a difficult-to-visualize configuration of fretting-hand fingers, fingering diagrams can be helpful. Your attention will be called to each diagram by a *reference mark* above the *tablature* staff. At the top of each diagram is a Roman numeral indicating the number of its topmost fret (I for first fret, IV for fourth fret, and so on). Here is the order of reference marks you will encounter in the tablature:

*, †, ‡, §, ¶, **, ††, ‡‡, §§, ¶¶ . . .

Making Music with the Fretting Hand

When a note is produced by some action of the *fretting* hand, it is connected to the preceding note in *both* tablature and standard notation by a *slur sign*. Slur signs look just like ties (see figure 2–11), but a tie connects two *identical* notes while a slur connects two *different* notes. The particular action performed by the fretting hand to obtain a note is then notated in *tablature* at the end of that note's stem, as follows:

      H - hammer-on

      P - pull-off

    SL - slide

H's and P's are, by convention, *not* written into standard notation, since these directions are immediately apparent from the context. The symbol "SL" appears in both tablature and standard notation. See Chapter 3 for a review of all three maneuvers.

THE CHOKE

A choke, or bent string, is notated in both tablature and standard notation by placing the symbol "ch" at the end of a choked note's stem. Chokes are also reviewed in Chapter 3.

Tempo Instructions (♩ =72, 𝅗𝅥 = 60)

The speed or *tempo* at which a tune is played can be suggested by metronome settings. The setting offered for each piece indicates the *approximate* speed at which an accomplished musician would play the tune. An acceptable speed for guitar students is about 80 to 90 percent of this figure. For instructions on how to use a metronome, see Appendix D.

Other Symbols and Directions

Here are some other symbols and directions you will encounter in the tablature and/or standard notation. Those symbols or directions introduced in *Fingerstyle Guitar* are reviewed here. Those introduced in this book are listed in figure 2–23.

REPEAT SIGNS

When part of a tune is repeated, repeat signs (see figure 2–19) appear in the tablature and standard notation. When you see a repeat sign with *dots on the left*, return to the nearest repeat sign with *dots on the right*. Then replay the entire intervening section.

Figure 2–19

FIRST AND SECOND ENDINGS

Sometimes a repeated section of a piece ends differently the second time through. Instead of printing the entire section twice, it is customary to use first and second endings, which are shown in figure 2–20. When you see this notation, play through the section up to the repeat sign with dots on the left, including the measure or measure

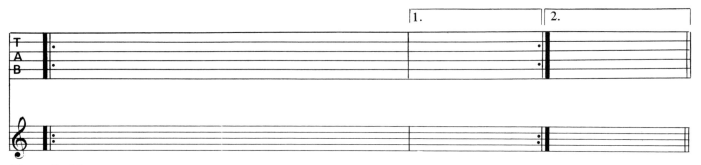

Figure 2-20

under bracket 1 (the *first ending*). Then return to the nearest repeat sign with dots on the right and replay the section. As you approach the end of the section, however, skip the first ending and play the measure or measures under bracket 2 (called the second ending). Then go on to the next section.

THE ACCENT SYMBOL

When a note gets a special *accent* (emphasis), it is marked with an accent symbol, shown in figure 2-21.

>

Figure 2-21

THE BROKEN CHORD OR ROLL SIGN

This symbol, shown in figure 2-22, indicates that an apparently simultaneous group of notes is to be played in rapid succession, instead of all at once.

Figure 2-22

DA CAPO AL FINE (D.C. AL FINE)

This direction often appears at the end of the notation for a piece. When you see it, return to the beginning and continue playing until you see the word *Fine*, which indicates the true ending of the tune.

NEW SYMBOLS AND DIRECTIONS

Figure 2-23 shows new symbols and directions introduced in this book. Alongside each entry is the page number where it is explained.

Figure 2–23

PLAYING DIRECTIONS		RHYTHM NOTATION	
I°, II°...	p. 36		p. 137
⌢	p. 38		p. 173
◇	p. 56		p. 173
▼	p. 77		
	p. 96		
ch	p. 151	**TUNINGS**	
I+, Barre II, +...	p. 166	E-A-D-F♯-B-E	p. 122
Rubato, a tempo	p. 172	D-A-D-G-A-D	p. 137
8ve	p. 174		

OTHER MARKINGS

⊕		p. 42
D.C. al ⊕e poi la coda		p. 42
𝄋		p. 83
D.S. al Fine		p. 83
D.S. al ⊕e poi la coda		p. 83

CHORD SYMBOLS

Fm	p. 38
Bm	p. 57
F♯	p. 57
C♯7	p. 82
F♯7	p. 101
B 9, F 9, B 13, F 13, F♯7♭5, F7♭9, F11, Cm7♭5, B♭11, B♭7♭9	p. 168
B9-II, F13-V...	p. 168

19

3

Fingerstyle Techniques

In this chapter, I'll review much of the technical material presented in *Fingerstyle Guitar*. If you need more detail, consult the index in that book for the location of the various explanations, examples, and exercises.

Fingerpicking Basics

The foundation of fingerstyle guitar is the alternating bass. The fretting hand stops a standard chord form, while the thumb of the plucking hand plays a *bass note* on each beat of every $\frac{4}{4}$ time measure. On the first and third beat of each measure, the thumb generally plays the *root note* of the chord. (The root note has the same letter name as the chord.) On the second and fourth beats of each measure, the thumb plays an *alternate note* of the chord on a different string. Most often, the root note is played on the fifth or sixth strings while the alternate note is played on the fourth string, as shown in figure 3–1.

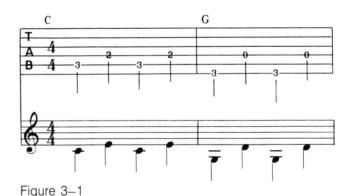

Figure 3–1

Notes on the *treble strings* (strings 1 through 3) are played by the fingers. Ordinarily, the index finger plays the third string, the middle finger plays the second string, and the ring finger plays the first string. Treble notes are either played as *pinches* (simultaneously) with bass notes or halfway between two bass notes, as shown in figure 3–2.

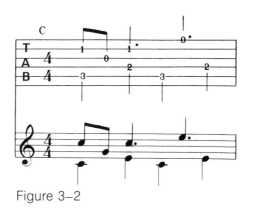

Figure 3–2

PATTERN PICKING

Also called Travis- and Cotton-picking, this is the fundamental fingerpicking accompaniment style. There are several widely used patterns. Each pattern has an alternating bass and some combination of pinches and between-beat treble notes. Some basic patterns are shown in figure 3–3.

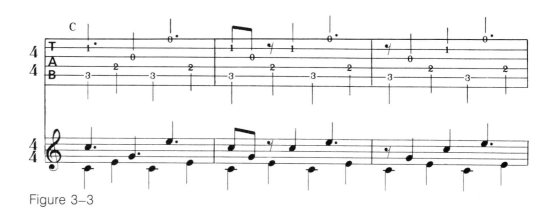

Figure 3–3

PLAYING MELODIES

Simple melodies can be obtained by "adding" melody notes to basic chord forms. While stopping a chord form such as C (figure 3–4a), a free finger frets an additional note (figure 3–4b), or a finger is removed from the form allowing an open string to be played (figure 3–4c), or a finger is removed from the form to play a note on a nearby string (figure 3–4d). These additional notes can be played instead of the ordinary treble notes of any pattern pick. Or they can be played directly over an alternating bass without reference to any particular pattern pick.

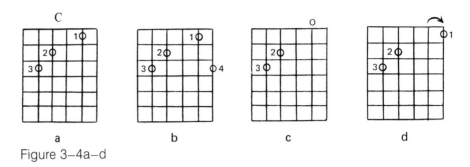

Figure 3–4a–d

Syncopation

Syncopation is an important feature of fingerstyle guitar. Briefly, syncopation means playing an accented note in a spot where notes are not ordinarily accented. In $\frac{4}{4}$ time, the note falling on the first beat of each measure is heavily stressed, while notes falling on each succeeding beat are lightly stressed. In many fingerpicking styles, the second and fourth thumb notes of each $\frac{4}{4}$ measure are stressed heavily. This produces a syncopated attack known as the *swing bass*. Many fingerpicking styles also call for many stressed between-beat notes, resulting in syncopated melodies. In fact, melody notes are often purposely moved by the player from on-beat to between-beat locations to increase the amount of syncopation in a tune.

SYNCOPATED CHORD CHANGES

When a note that has been syncopated (moved from an on-beat to a between-beat location) coincides with a chord change, that chord change must also be syncopated. In other words, if the note is played between beats, the chord change must also occur between beats. In figure 3–5, an open G-note was moved ½ beat back from the beginning of the second measure to the end of the first measure. The chord

Figure 3–5

change to C from F must be made at the moment that the open G-note is played—one-half beat before the start of measure 2.

Hammer-Ons

In a hammer-on, a fretting-hand finger strikes down sharply on a sounding string, producing an extra note by driving that string against the fingerboard. The technique is easily integrated into pattern picking, as shown in figure 3–6. Hammer-ons can begin between the beats, as shown in figure 3–7. They can be performed on thumb-plucked strings (figure 3–8a). When the plucked string of a hammer-on is fretted (figure 3–8b), keep enough pressure on the string so that the plucked note continues to sound until the hammering finger reaches the fretboard.

Other kinds of hammer-ons include the double-string H (figure 3–8c), where you pluck two strings and hammer on to both of them simultaneously with two different fretting-hand fingers; the double H, where you pluck one string and hammer on to two strings (figure 3–8d), and the alternate-string H, where you pluck one string and hammer on to *another* string (figure 3–8e).

Figure 3–6

Figure 3–7

Figure 3–8a–e

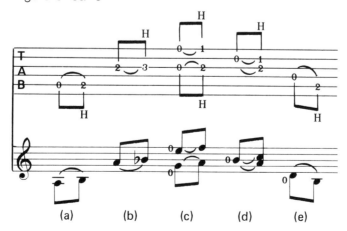

(a) (b) (c) (d) (e)

A pull-off begins with a plucked fretted string. Maintaining sufficient pressure to keep the string sounding, catch the edge of the string with the tip of your fretting finger and draw that finger in toward your palm in such a way that the string produces a clear note. Pull-offs are integrated into pattern picking as shown in figure 3–9. They can originate between beats, as shown in figure 3–10. They can be performed on thumb-plucked strings (figure 3–11a). When the P-note (the note produced by the pull-off) is fretted (figure 3–11, b and c), take care to fret both the plucked note and the P-note at the same time. Then pull off from the P-note fret to the plucked-note fret.

Figure 3–9

Figure 3–10

Figure 3–11a–c

Figure 3–12

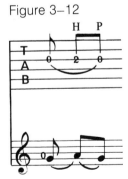

THE H-P COMBINATION

Pluck any string, hammer on to that string and keep it sounding. Then, using the hammering finger, pull off from that string without allowing a break in the sound. An H-P combination is shown in figure 3–12.

26

The Slide

In a slide, notes are produced by gliding with full pressure up (or down) a fretted sounding string. Slides can originate on the beat (figure 3–13) or between beats (figure 3–14). Slides can be performed on thumb-plucked strings (figure 3–15a). When a slide is more than one fret long (figure 3–15, b and c), care must be taken to relax pressure slightly as one moves over the intervening fretwires.

Two other kinds of slides you will encounter include the half-barre slide (figure 3–15d), where the flat underside of the first finger glides up one fret with full pressure on two or more strings, and the double-string slide (figure 3–15e), where a slide is performed simultaneously on two different strings with two different fingers. Observe that there is also a technique in which two strings are plucked, but a slide is performed in only one of them, as shown in figure 3–15f.

Figure 3–13

Figure 3–14

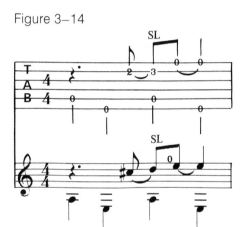

Figure 3–15a–f

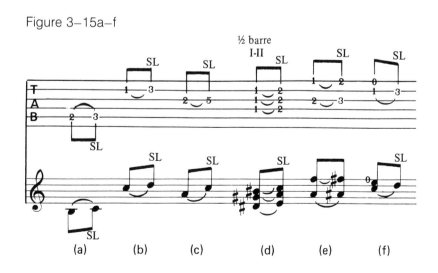

(a)   (b)   (c)   (d)   (e)   (f)

QUICK SLIDES

In a quick slide, the sliding finger begins to glide on a string the moment that string is plucked. A quick slide is written as a *grace note* (see figure 2–8), and it is actually an *ornament* (decoration) of the full-fledged note that follows, as shown in figure 3–16. (Observe that grace notes are played as pinches with bass notes but, by convention, they are written off to the left of the bass-treble alignment of full-fledged notes). All rules that apply to ordinary slides also apply to quick slides.

Figure 3–16

Chokes

In a choke, the pitch of a string is raised by pushing or bending that string at a given fret along the surface of the fingerboard (figure 3–17). Generally, the pitch of a string is raised to a point just short of what would be obtained by playing the next higher fret on the string. Strings 1 through 5 are generally choked out from the palm, but string 6 must be choked in toward the palm.

Figure 3–17

Triplets

A triplet is a group of three notes played in the space of one beat in $\frac{4}{4}$ time. There are numerous ways to obtain these in fingerstyle, some of which are shown in figure 3–18.

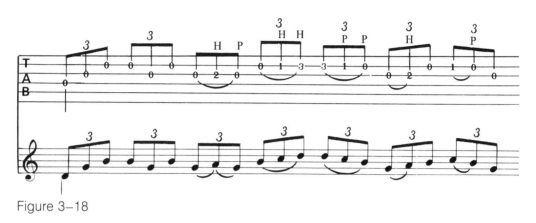

Figure 3–18

Grace Notes

Grace notes are very quick notes not officially allotted any time value of their own. Instead, they "borrow" a tiny amount of time from the next full-fledged note, and they are used to *ornament* (decorate) that full-fledged note. In fingerstyle, most grace notes are extra quick pull-offs. A fretted note is plucked, then pulled off almost instantly to the open string (figure 3–19a) or to a lower fret on that string (figure 3–19b). Observe that the grace note in figure 3–19c is played as a pinch with the bass note, even though it is written off to the left of the bass-treble alignment. All rules that apply to ordinary P's also apply to grace P's.

Figure 3–19a–c

(a)   (b)   (c)

DOUBLE GRACE NOTES

A double grace note is a pair of very quick notes that borrows a tiny amount of time from and ornaments the following full-fledged note. Most often, double grace notes are obtained in fingerstyle by means of very quick H-P combinations, as shown in figure 3–20, a and b. The notation in figure 3–20c indicates that the first note of the double grace note is played as a pinch with the bass note, even though it is written off to the left of the bass-treble alignment.

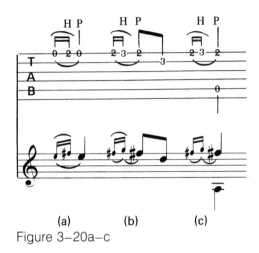

Figure 3–20a–c

The Advanced Plucking Hand

In basic fingerpicking, the thumb plays bass notes on strings 4, 5, and 6 (the *bass strings*) while the fingers play melody notes on strings 1, 2, and 3 (the *treble strings*). In more advanced playing, the thumb can play notes on the treble strings, and the fingers can play notes on the bass strings. When the fingers do play notes on the bass strings in a given passage, a special adjustment must be made.

When finger notes appear on the fourth string, the plucking hand is shifted so that the i finger can easily reach that string. Then the m finger plays notes on the third string, and the r finger plays notes on the second string. When finger notes appear on the fifth string, the plucking hand is shifted farther, where the i finger plays fifth-string notes, the m finger plays fourth-string notes, and the r finger plays third-string notes.

BASS RUNS

A bass run is a group of melody notes played on the bass strings by the thumb. Bass runs are ordinarily employed to fill in "spaces" (long notes or rests) in the treble melody, but sometimes they are played at the same time as portions of that melody. When two melodies (for example, a song melody and a bass run) are played simultaneously, the result is known as *counterpoint*.

THUMB-INDEX RUNS

A rapid *run* (series) of eighth notes can be obtained by alternating thumb- and index-finger strokes, as shown in figure 3–21. Thumb-index runs can be employed as bass-run fillers or serve as portions of a tune's melody line.

Figure 3–21

THE HARP EFFECT
(MELODIC FINGERING PATTERNS)

This technique requires some cooperation from the fretting hand. By combining the notes resulting from a simple fingering pattern with open-string notes (figure 3–22a), the plucking-hand fingers can obtain runs of adjacent melody notes by playing neighboring strings in succession, as shown in figure 3–22b. All these melody notes are then allowed to ring together somewhat, making the guitar sound like a harp.

Figure 3–22a

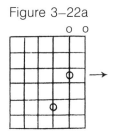

Figure 3–22b

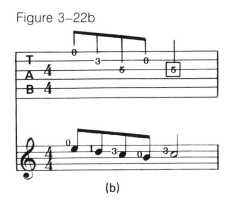

(b)

A number of problems arise when a guitarist first ventures up the neck. Some solutions are reviewed here.

EFFICIENT FINGERING

It is often difficult for the inexperienced player to come up with efficient fingering when confronted with a series of seemingly unconnected up-the-neck notes. One important aid is the *position notation* discussed in Chapter 2. With position notation, each finger is assigned a fret, no matter what string a note falls on.

When you need to stop simultaneously the same fret on more than one string, follow this rule: *The lower-number finger always plays the higher-number string*. So if you wanted to stop four strings on the same fret without barring, you would use the fingering shown in figure 3–23.

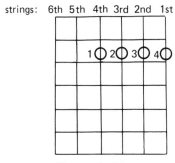

Figure 3–23

CUTTING STRINGS SHORT

You can avoid sloppy-sounding string noises when shifting positions by learning to *cut strings short*. To cut a string short, release pressure but don't take your fretting finger off the string until it has completely stopped sounding. Then release the string and shift quickly to the next position.

UP-THE-NECK BASS NOTES

Here are several ways to make the job of obtaining up-the-neck bass notes easier.

Open Tunings   In an *open tuning*, the guitar is actually tuned differently so that frequently used bass notes fall on open strings. The guitarist is then free to play melody up the neck without having to be overly concerned about fretted bass notes. Figure 3–24 shows instructions for obtaining from standard tuning the three open tunings introduced in *Fingerstyle Guitar*.

Figure 3–24

DROP-D TUNING (D-A-D-G-B-E)

• Tune string 6 down till the pitch of its seventh fret matches the open A string (Or, tune string 6 one *octave* below string 4).

OPEN-G TUNING (D-G-D-G-B-D)

• Tune string 6 as for Drop D tuning.

• Tune string 1 down till its pitch matches fret 3, string 2 (Or, tune string 1 one octave above string 4)

• Tune string 5 down till its pitch matches fret 5, string 6 (Or, tune string 5 one octave below string 3).

OPEN-D TUNING (D-A-D-F♯-A-D)

• Tune string 6 as for Drop-D tuning.

• Tune string 1 as for Open-G tuning.

• Tune string 3 down to match fret 4, string 4.

• Tune string 2 down to match fret 3, string 3 (Or, tune string 2 one octave above string 5).

Barres and Half Barres   Both barres and half barres (see Chapter 2) are effective ways of getting up-the-neck bass notes. Several strings (including bass strings) are fretted by the first finger, leaving the remaining fingers free to obtain melody notes or additional bass notes.

Barre Chords and Movable Chords   For both barre chords and movable chords (see Chapter 2), any fretted note that falls on a bass string can be used as a bass note.

Partial Chords   Portions of barre chords or movable chords can be moved up the neck and played in combination with open strings or thumb-fretted bass strings (see next paragraph). For more on this subject, see Chapter 4.

Thumb Fretting   The fretting-hand thumb can easily be used for pressing down the sixth string, leaving the other fretting-hand fingers free for stopping melody notes or additional bass notes on any of the other strings.

4

Alternating Bass Pieces

Fingerstyle Guitar explored alternating bass picking, but ultimately moved beyond the style to cover such areas as fiddle tunes and ragtime. In this chapter, I'll discuss many aspects of alternating bass picking left untouched in that book. More important, we'll begin to move away from the notion that fingerstyle has just two distinct parts—bass and melody.

Harmony

Briefly, harmony is a set of rules that determines which notes or chords make an effective accompaniment (musical background) for a given melody. A series of notes or *progression* (series) of chords that works as an accompaniment for a melody is known as the *harmony* of that melody. The art of creating such an accompaniment is called *harmonizing*. If you are not yet familiar with such basic aspects of music theory as notes, scales, and keys, see Appendix A before proceeding.

THE IMPORTANCE OF KNOWING THE HARMONY

In basic fingerstyle, a piece is presented as a series of chord forms. The player knows that all notes in a given form sound good together, and that effective bass notes can be found merely by playing the bass strings of that form. In more advanced playing, the familiar forms occur rarely, and the player must determine the harmony of a passage in order to know which notes to allow to sound together and which bass notes to use.

To help you learn about harmony, chord indications showing the harmony of each piece appear above the *standard notation staff*. Observe that the chord symbols appearing above the *tablature staff* are actually fingering aids. In other words, they indicate that a particular passage is played while stopping a basic form or barre form, such as the ones shown in figures 2–17 and 2–18.

Diminished Seventh Chords (I°, II°, . . .)

Diminished seventh chords appear frequently in a number of fingerpicking styles. Figure 4–1 (a and b) shows the two most frequently

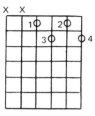

Figure 4–1a

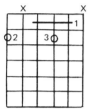

Figure 4–1b

used movable diminished seventh forms. The form called for in a given situation is always evident from the context. In tablature, the notation for these chords shows a Roman numeral above the staff (for fret location) plus the standard symbol for diminished chords—a small ° superscript. An indication above the standard notation staff shows the actual pitch of the chord. For more on diminished seventh chords, see 81, 117, and 159.

"Georgia Camp Meeting" is a late nineteenth century cakewalk. Camp meetings were large outdoor gatherings of evangelical Protestants. Cakewalk music, which was used on the plantation to accompany dance contests, is generally regarded as the ancestor of ragtime. Since the winner of each contest was awarded a piece of cake, the music became known as "walkin' fo' dat cake" or "cakewalk" music. An interesting version of the tune can be heard on *Dave Van Ronk and the Jug Stompers* (Mercury). Observe the diminished seventh chord in measure 13 and the harmony indications over the standard notation staff.

Georgia Camp Meeting

Standard tuning
Key: C major

♩ = 116

arranged by Ken Perlman

(continued)

TECHNIQUE[1]

Three fairly quick chord changes appear in measures 13–14—from F to I° (F♯°7), from I° to Am, and from Am back to F. This passage will flow much more smoothly if you make each change on the open G-note.

The Fermata

Figure 4–2

A *fermata* (figure 4–2) is placed over a note or simultaneous group of notes to indicate that the player should pause momentarily before proceeding. The length of the pause is up to the discretion of the player, but it generally should not exceed a beat or two.

The F Minor (Fm) Chord

Figure 4–3

Fm

The F minor form is shown in figure 4–3.

[1]Note that all "Technique" sections refer to the preceding tune.

The Blues Scale

The blues scale developed in the nineteenth century when black Americans adapted the major and minor scales (Appendix A) to music heavily influenced by African traditions. Blues scales are major scales that include, in addition to seven diatonic tones, certain *accidentals* (sharps, flats, or natural notes not in the original key) known as *blue notes*. These accidentals are:

- the note between the second and third notes of a major scale
- the note between the sixth and seventh notes of a major scale
- the note between the fourth and fifth notes of a major scale

Here are the three most common key of C blues scales:

C - D - E♭ - E - F - G - A - B - C
C - D - E♭ - E - F - G - A - B♭ - B - C
C - D - E♭ - E - F - G♭ - G - A - B♭ - B - C

Pete Kairo

Pete Kairo, is a guitarist, guitar teacher, and all-around folk performer from the Boston, MA area who specializes in fingerpicking blues, ragtime, and fiddle tunes. He has performed at folk clubs, pubs, and festivals throughout the Northeast and has appeared in concert with, among others, Vassar Clements, Richie Havens, U. Utah Phillips, and Michael Cooney. His two albums, both on Physical World Records, are entitled *Playing It Safe* and *Hanging Out*.

Pete Kairo learned "Travelin' Man" from the playing of blues singer Pink Anderson (see *Pink Anderson: Medicine Show Man* on Prestige/Bluesville).[2] He arranged it in his own style with plenty of bass runs and a snazzy introduction. The song was originally performed in touring *medicine shows*, where comic songs and skits were used to draw crowds and help sell patent medicines. Note the counterpoints (simultaneous melodies and bass runs) in measures 5–6, 8–9, and 14–15 of the verse-chorus. Note also the Fm chord in the second ending. Fingering diagrams are shown in figure 4–4.

Figure 4–4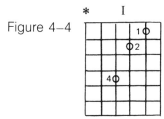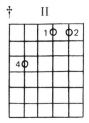

Travelin' Man

Standard tuning
Key: C major (blues scale)

arranged by Pete Kairo

♩ = 104

41

VERSE

I just wanna tell you bout a man named Coombs,
his home was in Tennessee,
He made his livin' stealing chickens and anything
he could see,
That hogeyed man he ran so fast he
hardly touched the road,
And if a freight train passed—no matter how fast,
he'd always get on bo'd.

CHORUS

He was a travelin' man, he cert'nly
was a travelin' man,
Trav-lin-est man, was ever in the land,
He traveled round, and he was known
for miles around,
He never got caught and never got whupped
till the pó-lice shot him down.

The Coda, The Proceed to Coda Sign,
D.C. al ⊕ e poi la coda

⊕

Figure 4–5

A *coda* or tag ending is a note, group of notes, or musical phrase tacked on to a piece to serve as the ending of that piece. Codas are needed when a piece has multiple verses or sections and no natural ending point.

When you see a "proceed-to-coda" sign (figure 4–5) above the staff, skip directly from that point to the coda on the last repetition of a tune. Sometimes, the instruction "D.C. al ⊕ e poi la coda" appears at the end of a tune. This means: Return to the beginning, play until you see the proceed-to-coda sign, then play the coda. If a part has repeat signs, wait for the second time through before going on to the coda.

The Drone Bass

In an alternating bass, the thumb hits different notes on different strings on each and every beat of a measure. In a *drone bass*, the thumb hits the same note (on the same string) on each and every beat of a measure. The note hit is usually the *tonic* note of the chord being used for harmony (the tonic, if you recall, is the note with the same letter name as the chord).

42

Thumb-Plucked Eighth Notes

You can add to the texture of a guitar arrangement by playing two thumb-plucked bass notes in the space of one $\frac{4}{4}$ time beat. This yields an interesting variation from the one-note-per-beat alternating or drone bass styles. To get your thumb limbered up for the task, practice any standard scale (see Appendix B) using only the thumb. Meanwhile, here's a short exercise to get you started.

Thumb-Plucked Eighth Note Exercise

Pete Seeger

Pete Seeger is perhaps our best known folk singer. He appeared on the scene in the late 1930s, was a companion of songwriter Woody Guthrie and blues singer Leadbelly (see "Silver City Bound" in Chapter 5), wrote the very first contemporary style folk music instruction book (*How to Play the 5-String Banjo*), and was a founding member of the Weavers.

Pete is usually associated with the banjo, which he has played since 1935, but he is also quite adept on 6- and 12-string guitar, having been strongly influenced by the percussive style of Leadbelly. He has recorded more than 80 albums, among the most recent of which are:

> *Singalong* (Folkways)
>
> *Circles and Seasons* (Warner Bros.)
>
> *Arlo Guthrie & Pete Seeger: Precious Friend* (Warner Bros.)
>
> *The Weavers: Together Again* (Loom)

Nowadays, Pete performs frequently around the world and is active in a variety of political and environmental causes. One of his major concerns—the preservation of New York State's Hudson River—has

Living in the Country

Tune sixth string to D
Key: D major

♩ = 138

by Pete Seeger

44

D.C. al ⊕ e poi la Coda

Coda

led to a longstanding association with the sloop Clearwater, which promotes conservation each year through a series of spring and summer concerts at Hudson River ports of call.

"Living in the Country" is a guitar "instrumental" written by Pete Seeger in the early 1960s that first appeared on his album *The Bitter and the Sweet* (Columbia).[3] "I was listening to my sister Peggy

[3]"Living in the Country," by Pete Seeger. © copyright 1962, 1963 by Fall River Music Inc. All rights reserved. Used by permission.

playing 'Pay Me My Money Down' (an Afro-American song from the Georgia Sea Islands)," writes Pete, "and later found myself improvising a new melody similar to it." Note the drone bass in part B, measures 3–4, part C, measures 5–7, and the coda; note also the thumb-plucked eighth notes in part B, measure 8 (first ending). Fingering diagrams for the tune are shown in figure 4–6.

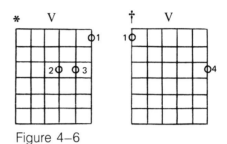

Figure 4–6

TECHNIQUE

A *Big Stretch*   Start out part A, measure 1, by assuming the fingering form marked with an asterisk in figure 4–6. Begin stretching your fourth finger out almost immediately and, at a point halfway through beat 2 of the measure, cut all the strings in the form short (see Chapter 3), release the fingering form, and leap up with your pinky to stop fret 10, string 1 (high D). Then glide down on the fourth string to fret 9, string 1 (high C♯) and fret 7, string 1 (high B).

Changing Rapidly from the A Form to the D Form   In part C, measures 5–8, you are asked to make several quick changes from the A chord to the D chord and vice versa. Treat these as if they were syncopated chord changes (Chapter 3) and make each change on the last half beat of the measure, coinciding with the playing of the middle-A note (fret 2, string 3). If you use the fingerings shown in figure 2–17, it will be a simple matter for you to pivot on the first finger (which stops middle A in both forms) and move just the second and third fingers back and forth between chords.

Multiple Operations on the Same String

In an H-P combination (Chapter 3), three notes can be obtained from a single plucked string (a plucked note, an H-note, and a P-note). Many such multiple operations are possible. "Brown's Ferry Blues," for example, contains two double hammer-slide (H-SL) combinations in which you hammer on to two strings at once with two different fingers. Then without relaxing pressure, you slide both fingers up one fret. Also present in the tune is a hammer-slide-pull-off (H-SL-P) combination. Here, start with an H-SL and, maintaining full pressure, pull off the string with the sliding finger.

"Brown's Ferry Blues" is one of the best-known songs performed by the Delmore Brothers, who were stars of the Grand Ole Opry during the 1930s and 1940s (see *The Delmore Brothers: Brown's Ferry Blues*, on County).[4] Alton Delmore played a flatpicked rhythm guitar style filled with short tasty licks and bass runs, while Rabon Delmore played lead (melody) parts on tenor (four-string) guitar. In recent years, their songs have been recorded by many bluegrass and folk music notables, such as Flatt and Scruggs, Doc Watson, and Norman Blake. Note the H-SL combinations in measures 5 and 13 and the H-SL-P combination in measure 15. Fingering diagrams appear in figure 4–7.

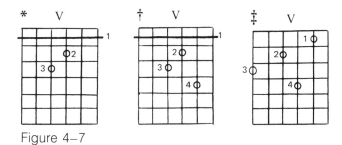

Figure 4–7

LYRICS

Hard luck poppa countin' his toes,
You can smell his feet wherever he goes,
Lord, Lord got those Brown's Ferry blues.
Hard luck poppa can't do his stuff
Trouble with him he's been too rough
Lord, Lord got those Brown's Ferry blues.

[4]"Brown's Ferry Blues," by Alton Delmore. © 1942 by American Music, Inc., renewed 1969 by Mrs. Alton Delmore, assigned to Vidor Publications, Inc.

Brown's Ferry Blues

Standard tuning
Key: A major (blues scale)

♩=112

by Alton Delmore
arranged by Ken Perlman

48

TECHNIQUE

Riding Down the Strings   At the end of measure 2, you are asked to switch from the barre-V form shown in figure 4–7 (marked with an asterisk) to a D7 form. Note that in both forms, the second finger stops string 3. To get this change smoothly, cut the last bass note of measure 2 short (see Chapter 3) and, having removed the first and third fingers from the fretboard, *ride* (glide noiselessly) on the second finger down string 3 from fret 6 to fret 2 (C♯ to A). Then use the second finger to pivot your thumb and first finger into the D7 form.

Interpreting Sixteenth Notes

As you know, sixteenth notes are defined as having 1/4 beat each in $\frac{2}{4}$, $\frac{3}{4}$, or $\frac{4}{4}$ time (figure 2–8). So two sixteenth notes make 1/2 beat and take up the space of one eighth note; four sixteenth notes make one beat and take up the space of one quarter note, and so on. Sixteenth notes are counted 1-a-&-a, 2-a-&-a, 3-a-&-a, 4-a-&-a, and so on.

Breaks

A break is an instrumental interlude between verses of a song. It has the same length, harmony, and overall feel as the original song, but the notes are often altered somewhat to form what is known as a *variation* on the melody. Breaks can be prepared in advance or *improvised* on the spot.

Dave Van Ronk

Dave Van Ronk was one of the first and most successful urban blues revivalists. His playing style, noted for its precision and excellent tone, has been emulated by thousands of would-be fingerpickers. His guitar arrangements—like the classics "Cocaine Blues" (see *Fingerstyle Guitar*) and "Come Back Baby"—are known for their originality and economy. Among his numerous albums are:

> *Dave Van Ronk Sings the Blues* (Verve Folkways)
>
> *Dave Van Ronk, Folksinger* (Prestige/Folklore)
>
> *Just Dave Van Ronk* (Mercury)
>
> *Inside Dave Van Ronk* (Prestige/Folklore)

Dave grew up in Brooklyn. His grandmother, who liked to sing, taught him "an assorted grab bag of Irish and American popular music, traditional and otherwise, dating from the middle of the nineteenth to the beginning of the twentieth century." He took up the banjo at 13, and over the next few years played Dixieland jazz in a number of bands. He switched to guitar in his late teens and learned to play by watching Greenwich Village denizens like Tom Paley and Eric Weissberg. He then spent years studying the recordings of old-time blues guitarists like Furry Lewis, Lightnin' Hopkins, Blind Boy Fuller, and Leadbelly.

Nowadays, Dave still lives and teaches guitar in Greenwich Village, occasionally embarking on long performance tours of the United States and western Europe. His latest album, *Somebody Else, Not Me*, is on Philo Records.

"Sunday Street" is the title cut from one of Dave Van Ronk's recent albums.[5] It combines recognizable elements from the styles of many old blues guitarists, but the result is pure Van Ronk. Dave plays the numerous adjacent double-string treble notes (for example, the two treble notes in the pickup measure), by brushing up on both of them with his index finger. They can also be played by two separate plucking-hand fingers. Do *not* play the lower of these two notes with the thumb, which should be confined to alternating bass duty. Dave uses a number of strange-looking fingering forms in this tune, many of which are shown in figure 4–8. Follow the harmony in the breaks by watching the indications above the standard notation staff.

VERSE

Not a dollar, not a nickel, not a penny to my name,
I'm the king of Tap City and I'm out of the game,
A nickel up, a nickel down, another nickel gone,
Ain't got a nickel left to carry me on,
If I ever get back on my feet,
I'll move from Saturday alley up to Sunday Street.

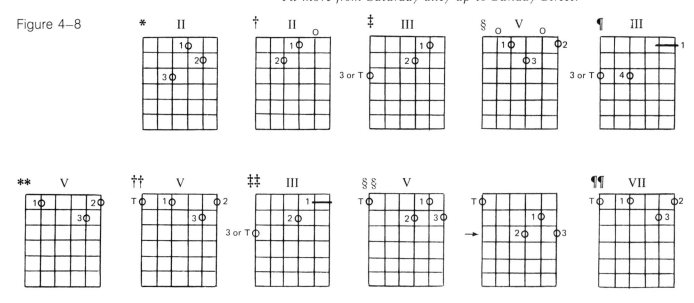

Figure 4–8

[5]"Sunday Street" by Dave Van Ronk, copyright © 1976 by Folklore Music, ASCAP.

Sunday Street

Tune sixth string to D
Key: D major (blues scale)

♩ = 120

by Dave Van Ronk

(continued)

52

TECHNIQUE

Fitting in Sixteenth Notes   A pair of sixteenth notes appears at the end of both measures 4 and 5 of the intro. & verse. To get the right sound, you must divide the last half beat of each measure (the time ordinarily occupied by one eighth note) exactly in half and play two 1/4 beat notes in that space. Figure 4–9 shows rhythm notation and counting for the treble part of measures 4 and 5.

Count: 1 & 2 & 3 & 4 a & a | 1 & 2 & 3 & 4 a & a |

Figure 4–9

"Blue Railroad Train" is another well-known tune by the Delmore brothers.[6] It can be heard on their *Brown's Ferry Blues* album (County). The melody of Alton Delmore's flatpicked bass runs on the original recording is recreated in the thumb-index runs of measures 8 and 9 of the intro. & break. Fingering diagrams appear in figure 4–10.

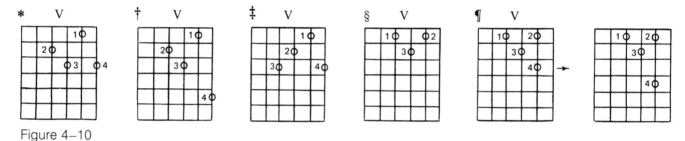

Figure 4–10

VERSE

Blue railroad train
Goin' down the railroad track
It makes me feel so doggone blue
To listen to that old smokestack.

Come back again
Let me hear the whistle blow
You're takin' the sun and leavin' the rain
And I hate to see you go.

Blue Railroad Train

Standard tuning
Key: E major (blues scale)

♩ = 108

by Alton Delmore
arranged by Ken Perlman

(continued)

TECHNIQUE

Obtaining Stretched Out Fingering Forms   In measure 3 of the intro. & break, you are asked to play the form shown in the dagger-marked diagram of figure 4–10, which calls for a five-fret stretch. To get the extra stretch you'll need for this maneuver, thrust your arm and your wrist forward without tensing your shoulder or pushing your elbow out from your side. This will have the effect of bringing the palm of your fretting hand virtually parallel to the fingerboard, freeing your fingers to stretch out to their maximum extent. When such extreme stretches are no longer required, bring your arm and wrist back to normal position. Do *not* leave your wrist thrust out for extended periods of time, since this can cause tendon strain.

Harmonics (Tablature Symbol: ◇)

Harmonics are bell-like tones produced by touching (rather than pressing down) a plucked string at a point that divides its length neatly into a fraction (one-half, one-third, one-quarter, and so on). The strongest harmonic on any string is obtained by placing a fretting-hand finger directly *over the wire* that borders the upper end of its twelfth fret, a point that divides the string exactly in half. If you then pluck this string, you will hear the beginnings of a bell-like tone. As soon as you hear this tone, remove your finger quickly from the string and the harmonic will ring out. The pitch of this harmonic is exactly one octave above the pitch of the open string.

Other frequently used harmonics occur at the wire bordering the upper end of the seventh fret (dividing the string in three) and at the wire bordering the upper end of the fifth fret (dividing the string in four). The sound of the seventh-fret harmonic on any string is one octave above the stopped seventh fret on that string. The sound of the fifth-fret harmonic is two octaves above the open string.

Harmonics are notated in tablature by placing a hollow diamond alongside a stem, as shown in the upper staff of figure 4–11. Observe that half barre and barre harmonics can be obtained by touching two or more strings at the wire bordering the upper end of the fifth, seventh, or twelfth frets with the flat underside of the first finger.

Figure 4–11

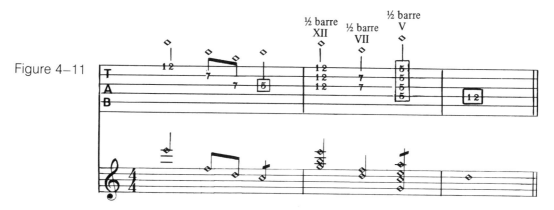

Harmonics are indicated in standard notation by changing the ordinarily round shape of a note or notes into hollow diamond shapes, as shown in the lower staff of figure 4–11. By convention, each diamond-shaped note indicates the fret at which a harmonic is obtained, *not* the actual pitch of the harmonic. Any doubts concerning which fret on the instrument is called for by a particular harmonic notation can be quickly resolved by a glance at the corresponding tablature staff. Harmonic pitches without stems are whole notes, while harmonic pitches with stems are quarter notes, eighth notes, and so on, as indicated. Harmonic half notes in standard notation have a slanted line cutting through a quarter-note stem.

The B Minor (Bm) and F♯ Chords

The basic forms for the Bm and F♯ chords are shown in figure 4–12.

Figure 4–12

An *interval* is the musical distance within a diatonic scale (see Appendix A) between any two pitches. The smallest interval is the distance from a note to itself, called a *first* or more commonly a *prime*. The distance from any pitch to a note one scale *step* higher (A-B, C-D) or lower (A-G, C-B) is called a *second*; the distance from any pitch to a note two scale steps higher (A-C, C-E) or lower (A-F, C-A) is called a *third*, and so on. Figure 4–13 shows the basic intervals. Observe that notes accompanied by a prime mark(′) are in a higher octave.

Figure 4–13

		EXAMPLES	
INTERVAL	SCALE STEPS APART	UP	DOWN
prime	—	A - A	D′ - D′
second	1	A - B	D′ - C
third	2	A - C	D′ - B
fourth	3	A - D	D′ - A
fifth	4	A - E	D′ - G
sixth	5	A - F	D′ - F
seventh	6	A - G	D′ - E
octave	7	A - A′	D′ - D

MAJOR, MINOR, PERFECT, AUGMENTED, AND DIMINISHED INTERVALS

All-natural-note diatonic scales are composed of a series of half steps and whole steps (see Appendix A). Specifically, the notes E and F, B and C are only a half step (one fret) apart, while all other notes are a whole step (two frets) apart. In other words, the distances B-C and E-F are smaller than the distances C-D and F-G, yet all are considered *seconds*; the distances B-D, E-G (three frets) are smaller than the distances C-E, F-A (four frets), yet all are considered thirds, and so on (see figure 8–1). Similarly, sharps and flats are *not* counted in determining the interval between two pitches. A-C is considered a third, but so is A-C♯, Ab-C♯, and so on.

To take account of all these different situations, musicians use the *intervalic modifiers* listed in the previous heading. Each modifier implies an *absolute distance* between two pitches, indicating that they are a specific number of half steps (frets) apart. For example, E-F, B-C, C-D♭, and F♯-G (one half step apart) are considered *minor* seconds, while E-F♯, B-C♯, C-D, F-G (one whole or two half steps apart) are considered *major* seconds. E-G, B-D, C-E♭, F♯-A (three half steps apart) are considered minor thirds, but E-G♯, B-D♯, C-E, F-A (two whole or four half steps apart) are considered major thirds, and so on.

Figure 4–14

MODIFIED INTERVAL	DISTANCE IN FRETS	EXAMPLES	
		UP	DOWN
perfect prime	0	A - A	D' - D
augmented prime	1	A - A♯	D' - D♭
minor second	1	A - B♭	D' - C♯
major second	2	A - B	D' - C
minor third	3	A - C	D' - B
major third	4	A - C♯	D' - B♭
diminished fourth	4	A - D♭	D' - A♯
perfect fourth	5	A - D	D' - A
augmented fourth	6	A - D♯	D' - A♭
diminished fifth	6	A - E♭	D' - G♯
perfect fifth	7	A - E	D' - G
augmented fifth	8	A - E♯	D' - G♭
minor sixth	8	A - F	D' - F♯
major sixth	9	A - F♯	D' - F
diminished seventh	9	A - G♭	D' - E♯
minor seventh	10	A - G	D' - E
major seventh	11	A - G♯	D' - E♭
perfect octave	12	A - A'	D' - D

Figure 4–14 shows some frequently encountered modified intervals. Observe that two pitches the same absolute distance apart are considered different intervals if they are called different letter names. For example, a distance of four half steps is considered a major third if we call the notes A-C♯; the same distance is considered a diminished fourth if we call the notes A-D♭. Observe also that the pitch E♯ is found on the same fret as F-natural (♮) and that B♯ is found on the same fret as C♮.

Intervals and the Guitar

As you've probably guessed by now, the strings of the guitar are tuned in intervals. In standard tuning, low E-A, A-D, D-G, and B-high E are all tuned in perfect fourths, while G-B is a major third.

When the two notes of any modified interval are stopped on two different guitar strings, they form a distinct, recognizable pattern. This pattern is the same on any pair of strings tuned the same interval apart. In other words, if you determine the fingering pattern for a modified interval on one of the perfect-fourth pairs of strings (low E-A, A-D, D-G, and B-high E), that pattern will yield the same modified interval on any other pair. This pattern will, of course, be different on G-B, the major third pair of strings. I could easily devote half the book to modified interval patterns, but I'll confine myself here to a discussion of the two families of interval patterns most used by finger-pickers—thirds and sixths.

THIRDS

Figure 4–15a shows how minor thirds appear on the guitar. On the perfect fourth-tuned pairs of strings, all minor thirds are two frets apart. On the major third-tuned pair of strings, they are one fret apart. Figure 4–15b shows major thirds, which are all one fret apart on perfect fourth-tuned pairs, and, of course, on parallel frets on the major third-tuned pair.

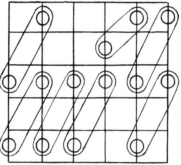

Figure 4–15a

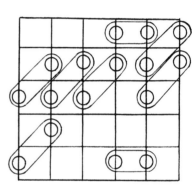

Figure 4–15b

SIXTHS

Sixths are usually obtained via skip-string pairs. Skip-string pairs that neither include nor cross the B-string (low E-D, A-G) have one fingering pattern for each kind of sixth, while those pairs that do include or cross the B-string (D-B, G-high E) have another fingering pattern.

Figure 4–16a shows how minor sixths appear on the guitar. On low E-D and A-G, they are all two frets apart. On D-B and G-high E, they are all one fret apart. Figure 4–16b shows major sixths, which

Figure 4–16a

Figure 4–16b

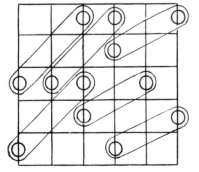

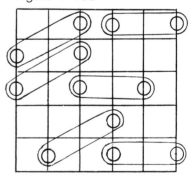

are all one fret apart on low E-D and A-G and which are on parallel frets on D-B and G-high E. (Observe that the open strings D-B and G-high E form major sixth intervals in their own right.)

THE SIGNIFICANCE OF THIRDS AND SIXTHS

Thirds are the building blocks of chords and often appear on their own in pieces in lieu of a full melody plus bass line. Sixths are *inverted* thirds (if the top note of any third is lowered an octave or the bottom note raised an octave, you get a sixth). Sixths also appear independently in guitar pieces. Whenever entities recognizable as thirds or sixths (figures 4–15 and 4–16) appear in guitar music, both strings should be stopped simultaneously, even when they are played separately.

THE THIRD VOICE

When thirds and sixths are used in conjunction with a base line, they allow for an intermediate part between the melody and bass, known to musicians as a *third voice*. This has the effect of beefing up the melody and creating a richer sound.

HARMONIZING

Any series of melody notes can be turned into a richer-sounding series of thirds or sixths. If the bottom note of a third is a melody note, the top note is known as a *third-above harmony*; if the top note of a sixth is a melody note, the bottom note is known as a *sixth-below harmony*, and so on.

Series of *diatonic thirds and sixths*, highly useful for harmonizing, can be constructed for each diatonic scale. Figure 4–17, measure 1, shows a C-major scale. In measure 2, each scale note is harmonized by another scale note a third above it; in measure 3, each scale note is harmonized by another scale note a third below it; in measure 4, each scale note is harmonized by another scale note a sixth above it; in measure 5, each scale note is harmonized by another scale note a sixth below it.

As you play through each series, you'll observe that some diatonic thirds and sixths are major while others are minor. Which thirds and sixths are minor or major is determined by the sequence within the scale of whole and half steps. In measure 2, for example, C-E is a major third, D-F is a minor third, E-G is minor, F-A is major, and so on. In measure 4, C-A is a major sixth, D-B is major, E-C is minor, F-D is major, and so on.

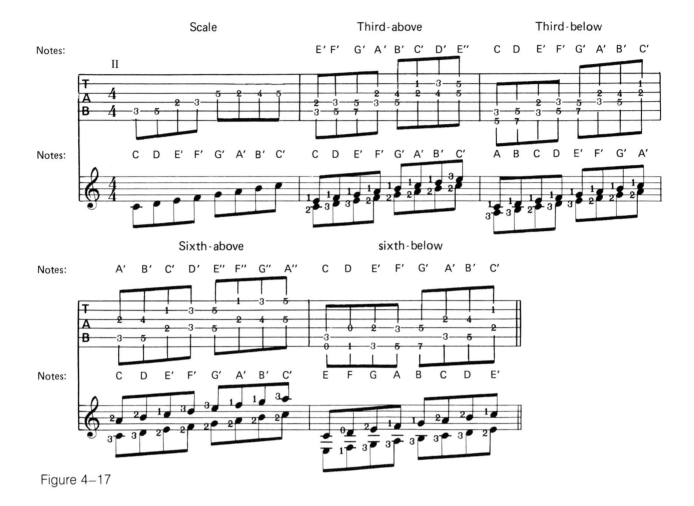

Figure 4–17

Janet Smith

Janet Smith is a guitarist and songwriter from Berkeley, CA. She has performed extensively at folk clubs and festivals in the western United States and in Italy, where she lived during the 1960s. She has two solo albums—*The Unicorn* (Takoma) and *I'm a Delightful Child* (Pacific Cascades)—and her playing appears on a number of anthologies, including *The Woman's Guitar Workshop* (Kicking Mule), *Berkeley Farms* (Folkways), and *Berkeley Out West* (Arhoolie). She has also worked as accompanist to noted songwriter Malvina Reynolds (see *Artichokes, Griddle Cakes, and Other Good Things*, on Pacific Cascades). Her musical collection, *Fingerstyle Guitar Solos*, has been published by Centerstream Music.

Janet took up the guitar in high school, after several years of piano lessons. She started off with ballad accompaniments in the Joan Baez style, but was soon drawn into solo playing, being particularly influenced by John Fahey and by Reverend Gary Davis (Chapter 5). She mentions Doc Watson, David Bromberg, Jorma Kaukonen and

Elizabeth Cotten as additional influences. Over the years, her interests have moved more and more in the direction of composition and orchestration. She now runs a small but thriving music copying and typesetting service in Berkeley called Bella Roma Music.

Janet Smith describes her composition "Piano Mover's Rag"[7] as "a modest venture into ragtime, using a few of the lighthearted devices that abound in the style." Janet mentions that she wrote the piece "while waiting for a piano mover to bring my trusty upright to my new apartment. He was unexpectedly on time, so the tune is rather short." The tune appears on the *Woman's Guitar Workshop* album and is printed in the April 1980 issue of *Guitar Player* magazine. Observe the thirds in measures 2–3, 11–12, and 18–19. Sixths appear in measures 3–4 of the second ending. Note the Bm chord and F# chords in measures 10 and 11 and the half-barre harmonic at the conclusion of the second ending.

Piano Mover's Rag

Standard tuning
Key: G major

by Janet Smith

(continued)

TECHNIQUE

Between Beat Thumb Notes In measures 1, 11–12, 17, and measures 2–4 of the second ending, you are asked to use the thumb to obtain between-beat melody notes—in most cases, the first note of a third or sixth. To get the right sound, count through each measure carefully (1 & 2 & 3 & 4 &), making sure that each thumb note falls exactly on the proper &-count.

Triads

Most basic chord forms are made up of three-note entities called *triads*. Triads are composed of two adjacent thirds sharing a middle note. For example, the adjacent thirds C-E and E-G form the triad C-E-G; the adjacent thirds G-B and B-D form the triad G-B-D, and so on. Major chords such as C major (C-E-G), G major (G-B-D), and D major (D-F♯-A) are triads in which a major third (C-E, G-B, D-F♯) precedes a minor third (E-G, B-D, F♯-A). Minor chords such as C minor (C-E♭-G), G minor (G-B♭-D), and D minor (D-F-A) are triads in which a minor third (C-E♭, G-B♭, D-F) precedes a major third (E♭-G, B♭-D, F-A). Diminished chords such as C° (C-E♭-G♭), G° (G-B♭-D♭), and D° (D-F-A♭) are triads made up of two minor thirds (C-E♭ + E♭-G♭, G-B♭ + B♭-D♭, D-F + F-A♭).

The initial note of each triad names the chord and is known as the *root* note, the middle note of each triad is called the *third* (it's a third above the root), and the final note of each triad is called the *fifth* (it's a fifth above the root). As it turns out, the "fifth" of a major or minor triad is a perfect fifth interval above the root, while the "fifth" of a diminished triad is a diminished fifth interval above the root (see figure 4–14). Figure 4–18 shows major and minor triads. Note that "♭♭" means *double flat* (twice flatted), that C♭ is found on the same fret as B♮ and that F♭ is found on the same fret as E♮.

Figure 4–18

TRIAD	MAJOR	MINOR	TRIAD	MAJOR	MINOR
C	C - E - G	C - E♭ - G	F	F - A - C	F - A♭ - C
G	G - B - D	G - B♭ - D	B♭	B♭ - D - F	B♭ - D♭ - F
D	D - F♯ - A	D - F - A	E♭	E♭ - G - B♭	E♭ - G♭ - B♭
A	A - C♯ - E	A - C - E	A♭	A♭ - C - E♭	A♭ - C♭ - E♭
E	E - G♯ - B	E - G - B	D♭	D♭ - F - A♭	D♭ - F♭ - A♭
B	B - D♯ - F♯	B - D - F♯	G♭	G♭ - B♭ - D♭	G♭ - B♭♭ - D♭
F♯	F♯ - A♯ - C♯	F♯ - A - C♯	C♭	C♭ - E♭ - G♭	C♭ - E♭♭ - G♭
C♯	C♯ - E♯ - G♯	C♯ - E - G♯			
G♯	G♯ - B♯ - D♯	G♯ - B - D♯			

TRIADS AND HARMONIZING

Any note in a triad can be played along with, or used as background for, any other note in the triad. So given a particular melody line, a knowledge of the *harmonizing triad* not only tells you which bass notes you can use, but lets you know what notes can be used between melody and bass to serve as a third voice (p. 61), or even a fourth voice, a fifth voice, and so on.

TRIADS, VOICINGS, AND THE GUITAR

Most of the basic triad forms played on guitar cover five or six strings (see figure 2–17). In addition to a simple triad, however, these forms repeat one or more of the triad notes at various octave levels. For example the C (major) form shown in figure 2–17 contains the pitches C-E′-G′-C′-E″; the G-major form contains the pitches G-B-D-G′-B′-G″, and so on.

The exact order of pitches at their various octave levels in a particular chord form is known as the *voicing* of that form. Many forms, each with its own voicing, are possible on guitar for each major and minor triad. Advanced fingerpicking requires not only the ability to recognize the different voicings called for in written music but also the art of making up original voicings when the need for them arises.

Voicings and Barre Chords

A thorough study of barre chords is a good place to start learning about chord voicings. Figure 2–18 reviews the basic barre forms, many of which are basic triad voicings played under a full barre. Each time you raise a barre chord up one fret, the pitch of that chord goes up a half step. For example, the barre E (major) form is an F major chord when played at the first fret, an F♯ (or G♭) major chord when played at the second fret, an A major chord at the fifth fret, a D major chord at the tenth fret, and so on. The barre Am form is a B♭ (or A♯) minor chord at fret 1, a B minor chord at fret 2, a D minor chord at fret 5, and so on.

As it turns out, each major and minor triad appears several times on the fingerboard, each time in the guise of a different barre chord form. And each new barre form is actually a radically different voicing for the given triad. For example, voicings for the triad A major occur at barre G-II (barre G played at the second fret), barre E-V, barre D-VII, and barre C-IX. Voicings for the E minor triad occur at barre Dm-II, barre C♯m-III, and barre Am-VII. Figure 4–19 shows the barre voicings for a number of common triads.

Figure 4–19

MAJOR CHORD	BARRE LOCATIONS	MINOR CHORD	BARRE LOCATIONS
C	A-III, G-V, E-VIII, D-X	Am	Em-V, Dm-VII, C♯m-VIII
G	E-III, D-V, C-VII, A-X	Em	Dm-II, C♯m-III, Am-VII
D	C-II, A-V, G-VII, E-X	Bm	Am-II, Em-VII, Dm-IX C♯m-X
A	G-II, E-V, D-VII, C-IX	F♯m	Em-II, Dm-IV, C♯m-V, Am-IX
E	D-II, C-IV, A-VII, G-IX	C♯m	Am-IV, Em-IX, Dm-XI
B	A-II, G-IV, E-VII, D-IX	Dm	Am-V, Em-X
F	E-I, D-III, C-V, A-VIII, G-X	Gm	Em-III, Dm-V, C♯m-VI, Am-X
B♭	A-I, G-III, E-VI, D-VIII, C-X	Cm	Am-III, Em-VIII, Dm-X, C♯m-XI
		Fm	Em-I, Dm-III, C♯m-IV, Am-VIII

BARRE VOICINGS
AND PARTIAL CHORDS

In *Fingerstyle Guitar,* I spoke of *partial chords*—parts of basic or barre forms that can be played up the neck in combination with open strings or thumb-fretted bass notes. By taking segments from any of the barre voicings listed in figure 4–19, you can easily construct your own partial chords. A knowledge of the notes occurring in each triad (see figure 4–18) then tells you which open notes or additional fretted notes are available to you. Since the triad E major, for example, is made up of the notes E, G♯, and B, E major voicings can use both open E-strings, the open B-string, and any fretted E's, G♯'s, and B's that are within reach.

The first column in figure 4–20 shows the barre-C voicing of the E major triad, along with two partial chords that are derived from it. Observe that open low E can be used as a bass note and that open high E or B can be used as treble notes. Each combination of open and fretted notes has its own distinct sound. The second column shows the barre-E voicing of the A major triad (A-C♯-E), along with two partial chords. Here, the open low E- and open A-strings can be used as bass notes and high E can be used for melody. Or, if desired, the thumb can stop a fret 5, string 6 (low A) bass note. The fifth column

Figure 4–20

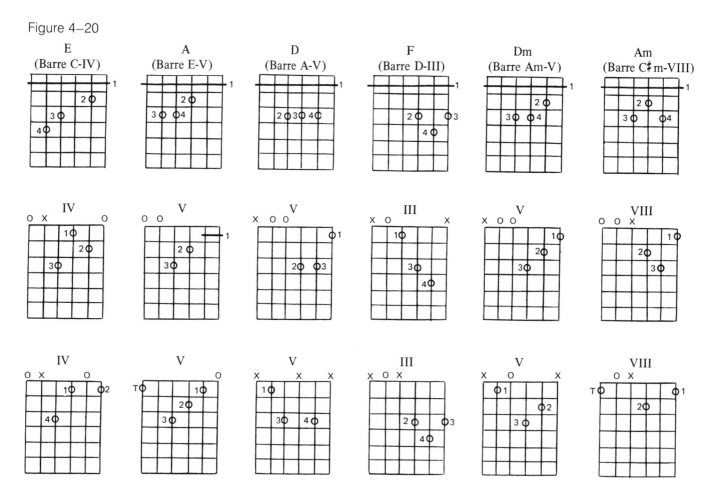

shows the barre-Am voicing of the Dm triad (D-F-A), for which the open D- and A-strings can be used as bass notes.

The Blues Turnaround

The blues turnaround is a run of notes designed to take you from the end of one blues verse to the start of another. Blues turnarounds usually follow one of a small number of fairly standard and easily recognizable patterns, often involving a series of descending thirds or sixths.

"Careless Love" is a late nineteenth century blues song about the pitfalls of romance. It has been recorded countless times by artists as diverse as Burl Ives and Dave Van Ronk (see *Dave Van Ronk: Gambler's Blues*). This arrangement is constructed primarily of partial chords and sixths. Measures 1 and 13 move from a partial barre D-II (E triad) to a basic E form. Measures 2 and 14 employ a partial barre A-II form (B triad). Measure 5 moves from a partial barre D-II (E triad) to a partial barre E-V (A triad), measures 7 and 8 employ a partial barre E-VII (B triad), measure 11 goes from a partial barre D-VII to a partial barre E-V (both A triads), and so on. Note the blues turnaround in measures 15 and 16. Follow the harmony above the standard notation staff (altered compound chords like "B13♭9" are explained in Chapter 7). Fingering diagrams appear in figure 4–21.

LYRICS

Love oh love oh careless love,
Love oh love oh careless love,
Love oh love oh careless love,
See what careless love can bring.

Figure 4–21

 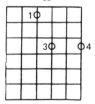 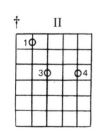 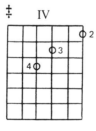 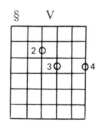 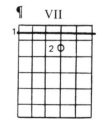 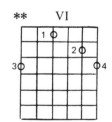

 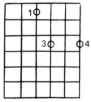 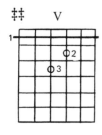

69

Careless Love

Standard tuning
Key: E major (blues scale)

♩ = 104

arranged by Ken Perlman

Daily Fingerpicking Exercises

Some kind of daily limbering-up routine for the plucking hand is a good idea for both the student and the experienced player. Here's a series of not-too-boring plucking-hand exercises designed especially for fingerstyle. The idea behind them is simple. First, take a basic chord form (these exercises use E, B7, and C7, but any form will do). Play a simple picking pattern while stopping the form (measures 1–2 of exercise 1), then move the form up a fret and repeat the pattern (measures 3–4 of exercise 1). Move the form up another fret (measures 5–6 of exercise 1) and repeat the pattern, move it up still another fret (measures 7–8 of exercise 1) and repeat the pattern, and so on up the neck until you run out of reachable frets. At each fret, the combination of fretted and open strings yields an interesting but unpredictable combination of harmonies and dissonances that reminds me very much of the playing of such present-day fingerpickers as John Fahey and Leo Kottke. Since the actual pitches played are unimportant, I've presented the exercise in tablature only.

Daily Fingerpicking Exercises

Exercise 1

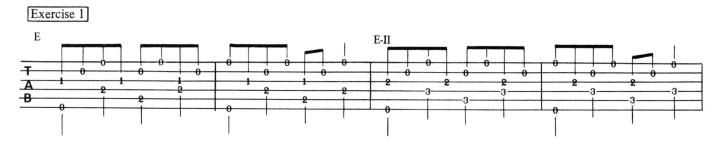

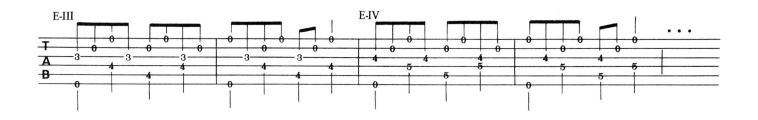

Exercise 2

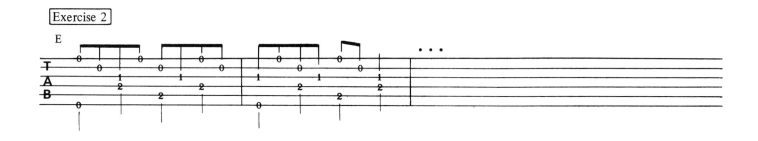

Exercise 3

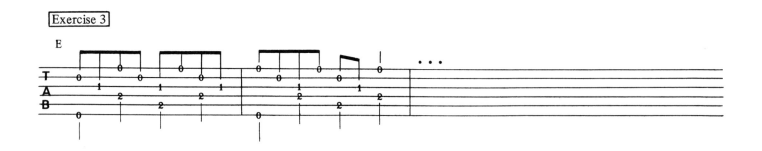

Exercise 4

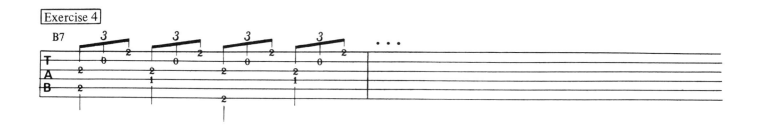

Exercise 5

Exercise 6

Exercise 7

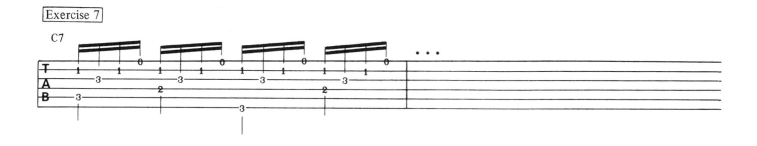

Exercise 8

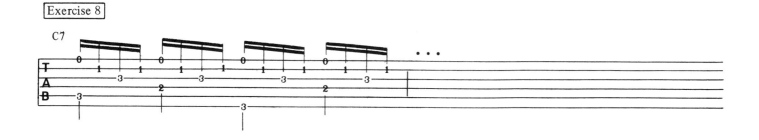

5
The Country Blues

Just about all present day nonclassical fingerpicking guitar styles owe their origin to country blues picking. The guitar was primarily a parlor instrument in this country until the early 1900s, when improved technology permitted the use of steel strings. The steel-string guitar spread, among other places, throughout the rural South where it was adopted by black blues singers as an ideal accompaniment tool. These blues singers took rhythms, conventions, and melodic ideas from their own musical traditions and combined them with a smattering of conventional guitar techniques. The result is what we now call *country* (that is, rural) blues.

Country blues playing styles varied widely from region to region, but they had a number of basic features in common. First, country blues guitar was almost always characterized by a steady bass supplied by the thumb. Initially, the thumb merely brushed over the bass strings, but as players became more sophisticated, they adopted the drone bass, the alternating bass, or a mixture of both.

The treble strings in country blues guitar were used for syncopated rhythmic ideas or melody. At first, rhythms were merely brushed up on two or more treble strings with the index finger. In more sophisticated playing, complex melodies and rhythms were plucked on single or multiple treble strings by two or even three plucking-hand fingers.

All country blues styles featured a number of techniques and conventions designed to help adapt the guitar to the African-descended blues sound. We've already discussed the blues scale, which added one or more accidentals (blue notes) to the notes of a major or minor scale. Blues guitarists also experimented with ways of obtaining tones that did not exactly correspond to fretted notes—that were, in effect, between two frets in pitch. These techniques included playing blue notes over major-triad harmonies, choking the strings, (see Chapter 3), and, in some styles, using a heavy glass or metal *slide* to stop the strings. (Since a slide can stop a string without pressing it down into the fingerboard, it produces between-fret tones when placed between fretwires).

After about 1920, country blues music went in two directions. Some players, like Blind Blake (p. 78), Mississippi John Hurt (see *Mississippi John Hurt: 1928 Sessions* on Yazoo), Blind Willie McTell (see *Blind Willie McTell: The Early Years* on Yazoo) and Reverend Gary Davis (see *Reverend Gary Davis* on Yazoo) brought their music closer to the American mainstream—with what most of us would call accessible melodies and relatively regular rhythms. Elements of this style were later borrowed by country music artists like Merle Travis and Doc Watson and by folk singers such as Woody Guthrie, Pete Seeger, Tom Paxton, and Bob Dylan.

Other country blues artists, like Blind Lemon Jefferson (see *Blind Lemon Jefferson: 1926–9*, vols. 1 and 2 on Biograph), Charlie Patton (see *Charlie Patton, Founder of the Delta Blues* on Yazoo), and Robert Johnson (see *Robert Johnson, King of the Delta Blues*, on Columbia), developed a sophisticated but more African-oriented sound that is less accessible to modern audiences. It was this style, however, that evolved into the electric guitar-oriented *Chicago blues* sound of artists like B. B. King (see *B. B. King, Live at the Regal* on ABC-Paramount). And, it was Chicago blues guitar playing that formed the basis of the electric guitar style featured in contemporary rock music.

Many fingerpickers are discouraged from attempting tunes with a strong country blues flavor by scratchy recordings and poor, confusing notation. This chapter will give you an opportunity to explore the roots of fingerstyle guitar through the arrangements and compositions of some present-day players who have mastered the country blues idiom.

Staccato (Symbol in Tablature: ▼)

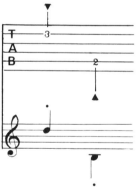

Figure 5–1

Staccato (stah-CAH-toe) is a musical term indicating that the ringing of a note is to be cut short (see Chapter 3). Staccato is indicated in tablature by placing a solid triangle next to a stem, as shown in the top staff of figure 5–1. In standard notation, staccato is shown by placing a dot next to a stem, as shown in the bottom staff of figure 5–1. The opposite of staccato is the term *legato* (leg-GAH-toe), which indicates that each note should run smoothly into the next note.

Stopping Two or More Strings, but Choking Only One

Figure 5–2

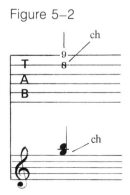

The trick here is to keep all the nonchoked strings so firmly pressed down that they stay put when the choked string is pushed out (no mean feat in most cases). This technique is indicated in tablature and standard notation as shown in figure 5–2, where a choke symbol ("ch") is connected by a slanted line to only one of two or more simultaneously played treble notes.

Rory Block

Rory Block is one of the best country blues guitarists and singers to emerge from the blues revival. She has performed throughout the United States, Canada, and western Europe, and she has shared the stage with such notables as Jerry Garcia, David Bromberg, Bonnie Raitt, John Sebastian, and Taj Mahal. She was the subject of a feature article in the November 1983 issue of *Guitar Player* magazine, and *Rolling Stone* praised her album *High Heeled Blues* (Rounder) as "some of the most singular and affecting country blues anyone—man or woman, black or white, old or young—has cut in recent years." Among her other albums are:

> *Intoxication* (Chrysalis)
>
> *You're the One* (Chrysalis)
>
> *Blue Horizon* (Rounder)
>
> *Rhinestones and Steel Strings* (Rounder)

The daughter of noted fiddler Allan Block (see *Alive and Well and Fiddlin'* on Living Folk), Rory was exposed to blues and traditional country music at an early age. She took up the guitar at 10, became interested in blues at 12, and was soon an enthusiastic participant at the frequent jam sessions held after hours at the Block Sandle Shop in the Greenwich Village district of New York City.

As a result of these sessions, she had the opportunity to meet and learn from a number of blues masters, such as Mississippi John Hurt, Son House, Skip James, Fred McDowell, and Bukka White. She also studied with Reverend Gary Davis. By the time she was 16, she was making note-for-note transcriptions of blues recordings, many of which were later used by Stefan Grossman in several blues instruction series. In 1966, she collaborated with Grossman on an album called *How to Play Blues Guitar*, which with its accompanying tablature book, has become one of the most influential guitar instruction packages.

In recent years, Rory has devoted considerable energy both to songwriting and to composing for guitar. She now lives in Chatham, NY.

Here's Rory Block's arrangement of "Police Dog Blues," a country blues standard.[1] The tune was first recorded by the great blues guitarist Blind Blake in the 1920s (see Blind Blake, *Bootleg Rum Dum Blues* on Biograph). Blake is believed to have grown up in Georgia, but he did most of his performing and recording in Chicago. His style is noted for its light, good-humored quality and for its precise rhythmic imitation of *stride* (honky-tonk) piano. Observe that the bass in

---

[1] "Police Dog Blues," arrangement © 1985 by Rory Block.

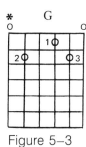

Figure 5–3

this piece is irregular. Sometimes there is no bass, sometimes a bass note is held for several beats. You'll have to do a lot of counting (1 & 2 & 3 & 4 & . . .) to get the right sound. Since the piece is in open D tuning (see Figure 3–24), I've presented a tablature version only. A fingering diagram appears in figure 5–3.

Police Dog Blues

♩ = 132

Tuning: D-A-D-F♯-A-D
Key: D major (blues scale)

arranged by Rory Block

(continued)

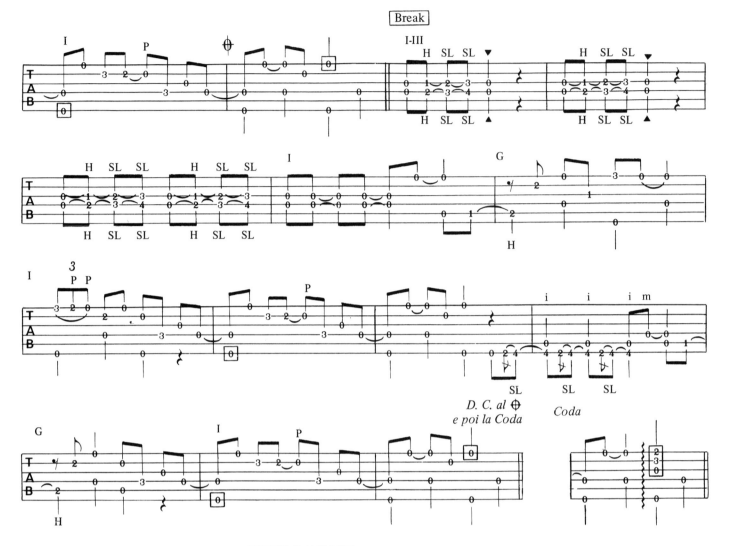

TECHNIQUE

A Downward Double Slide Followed by a Rest In measure 2 of the verse, you are asked to perform a downward slide on two strings at the same time, from fret 9, string 1 and fret 8, string 2 to fret 3, string 1 and fret 2, string 2. Immediately after the slide, a rest appears in the notation. To get the right sound, cut both notes short (Chapter 3) when you reach the end of your slide and quickly remove both fingers from the fretboard.

Cutting Open Strings Short In measures 1 and 2 of the break, staccato signs appear in relation to open strings. To cut open strings short, you must either lay the heel of your plucking hand on the strings, or you must place the tips of your fretting-hand fingers on the strings without exerting any pressure.

Quick Sliding on a Between-Beat Thumb Note This maneuver appears in measures 8 and 9 of the break. Exactly halfway through the fourth beat of measure 8, start a quick slide on string 6 from fret 2 to fret 4. Pluck open string 5 with i at the start of measure 10, start another quick slide half a beat later, and so on.

Seventh, Major Seventh, and Diminished Seventh Chords

Seventh chords are four-note entities consisting of a triad (Chapter 4) plus a *seventh interval* (that is, the note a seventh above the triad root). If the triad is major or minor and the interval is a major seventh (see figure 4–14), the result is called a *major seventh chord* (CMaj7, Gmaj7). If the triad is major or minor and the interval is a minor seventh, the result is usually referred to simply as a *seventh chord* (C7, Gm7). If the triad is diminished and the interval is a diminished seventh, the result is a *diminished seventh chord* (C°7, G°7). Be aware that when musicians use the term *seventh chords*, they are almost always referring specifically to *major and minor triads with added minor seventh intervals*.

All seventh, major seventh, and diminished seventh chords are made up of three adjacent thirds. Take any major triad (say C-E-G or C major) or minor triad (C-E♭-G or C minor), add on a major third (G-B), and the result is a major seventh chord (C-E-G-B or CMaj7, C-E♭-G-B or CmMaj7). Take any major or minor triad (say C or Cm), add on a *minor third* (G-B♭), and the result is a seventh chord (C-E-G-B♭ or C7, C-E♭-G-B♭ or Cm7). Take any diminished triad (say B-D-F or B°), add a *minor third* (F-A♭), and this yields a diminished seventh chord (B-D-F-A♭ or B°7).

As was the case for triads, any note in a seventh, major seventh, or diminished seventh chord—*including the added seventh note*—can be used to harmonize (become a bass note or added voice for) any other note in the chord. Any barred seventh forms (see figure 2–18) can be turned into partial chords in a manner similar to that suggested for triads (see figure 4–20). Figure 5–4 shows the notes that make up various major- and minor-based seventh and major seventh chords.

Figure 5–4   Seventh Chords

ROOT	MAJOR		MINOR	
	MAJ.-7	7	MAJ.-7	7
C	C - E - G - B	C - E - G - B♭	C - E♭ - G - B	C - E♭ - G - B♭
G	G - B - D - F♯	G - B - D - F	G - B♭ - D - F♯	G - B♭ - D - F
D	D - F♯ - A - C♯	D - F♯ - A - C	D - F - A - C♯	D - F - A - C
A	A - C♯ - E - G♯	A - C♯ - E - G	A - C - E - G♯	A - C - E - G
E	E - G♯ - B - D♯	E - G♯ - B - D	E - G - B - D♯	E - G - B - D
B	B - D♯ - F♯ - A♯	B - D♯ - F♯ - A	B - D - F♯ - A♯	B - D - F♯ - A
F♯	F♯ - A♯ - C♯ - E♯	F♯ - A♯ - C♯ - E	F♯ - A - C♯ - E♯	F♯ - A - C♯ - E
C♯	C♯ - E♯ - G♯ - B♯	C♯ - E♯ - G♯ - B	C♯ - E - G♯ - B♯	C♯ - E - G♯ - B
F	F - A - C - E	F - A - C - E♭	F - A♭ - C - E	F - A♭ - C - E♭
B♭	B♭ - D - F - A	B♭ - D - F - A♭	B♭ - D♭ - F - A	B♭ - D♭ - F - A♭
E♭	E♭ - G - B♭ - D	E♭ - G - B♭ - D♭	E♭ - G♭ - B♭ - D	E♭ - G♭ - B♭ - D♭

Arpeggios, Voice Leading, and the Walking Bass

When the notes of any chord are played in succession instead of all at once, the effect is known as an *arpeggio*. When the notes (voices) in a progression of chords are arranged so that the notes of one chord lead by the shortest possible distance into the notes of the next chord, the result is called *voice leading*. Voice leading shows up frequently on the guitar in the construction of an arpeggiated bass line known as a *walking bass*.

Suppose that a tune has a measure of G7 (G-B-D-F) followed by a measure of C (C-E-G). Figure 5–5 shows two possible walking bass lines that progress from G7 to C. Observe that the notes in the bass line outline a chord (that is, form an arpeggio) and that an attempt is made to have a minor-second interval (half step) whenever possible on the transition from chord to chord. To allow for a more interesting sound, walking bass lines frequently include scale notes and/or blue notes between arpeggio notes.

Figure 5–5

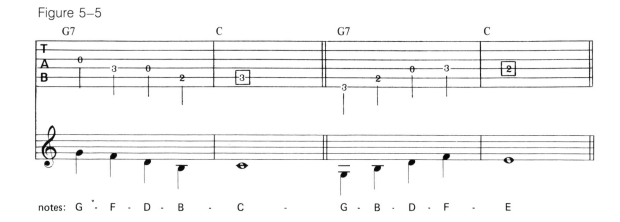

THE BOOGIE-WOOGIE BASS

A boogie-woogie bass is a walking bass made up primarily of seventh and diminished seventh chord arpeggios that progress from one to another by means of voice leading. Sometimes, a guitarist will play just a boogie bass throughout an entire verse of a tune, at which point the boogie bass becomes a *boogie break*.

The C♯7 Chord

The basic C♯7 chord is merely the fretted portion of a C7 chord (see figure 2–17) raised up to the second fret. The open E string is, of course, not part of the C♯7 form, but it is often added to the chord as a readily available and interesting dissonance.

The Segno, D.S. al Fine,
D.S. al ⊕ e poi la coda

𝄋

Figure 5–6

As you recall, D.C. al Fine (Chapter 2) directs you back to the beginning of a tune. When you need to return to any point other than the beginning, that point is marked with a *segno* (SEN-yo), shown in figure 5–6. So the notation *Dal Segno al Fine (D.S. al Fine)* means return to the segno and play until you see the word *Fine*. The notation *D.S. al ⊕ e poi la coda* means return to the segno, play until you see the return to coda sign, then play the coda.

Geoff Bartley

Geoff Bartley is a guitarist and singer-songwriter from Cambridge, MA. His playing style is a blend of country blues and chord-melody guitar (see Chapter 7) with a dash of acoustic rock-'n'-roll influence thrown in for seasoning. His album, entitled *Blues Beneath the Surface*, is on Magic Crow Records.

Geoff's first instrument was clarinet, but he took up the guitar in the early 1960s, when as he puts it, "the haunting ballads of early [Bob] Dylan weaned me from clarinet duets and Broadway soundtracks. Lightnin' Hopkins [see *Lightnin' Hopkins* on Archoolie] mesmerized me some years later with his dark hypnotic sound. Nowadays my playing still owes a great debt to this fierce Houston bluesman, but I try to arrange songs in my own style. In particular, I often try to make the guitar sound like a condensed jazz ensemble, complete with spare horn punches and walking bass."

Geoff Bartley arranged this version of "Bullfrogs on Your Mind," a song first recorded by Lightnin' Hopkins.[2] Hopkins was known for his exciting single-string blues runs and for the brooding intensity of his performances. This tune was one of Lightnin's more playful numbers, and Geoff's arrangement, which appears on his *Blues Beneath the Surface* album, emphasizes this aspect to the hilt. Geoff's break for the tune features a boogie-woogie bass with syncopated treble inserts to imitate a jazz horn section. An occasional walking bass quarter note is turned into two eighth notes for rhythmic variety. See figure 5–7 for fingering diagrams.

Figure 5–7   *   †

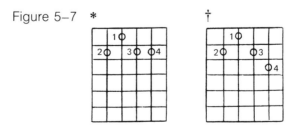

[2]"Bullfrogs on Your Mind," arrangement © 1984 by Geoff Bartley.

83

Bullfrogs on Your Mind

Standard tuning
Key: E major (blues scale)

♩ = 116

arranged by Geoff Bartley

(continued)

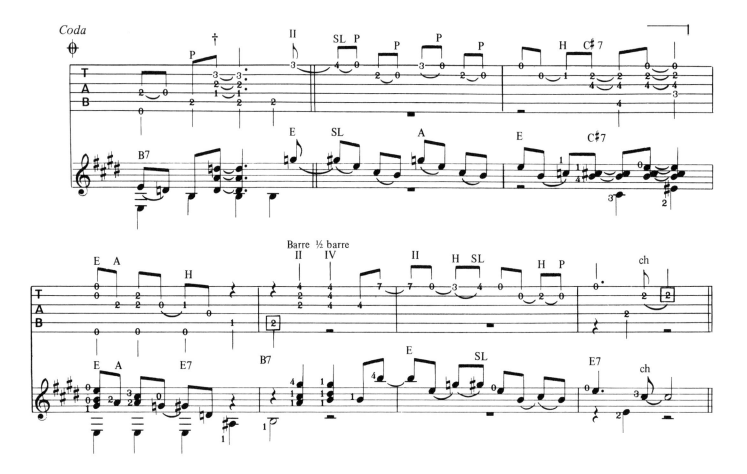

TECHNIQUE

Plucking Two Strings but Hammering On to Only One   At the transition from the intro. & verse to the break, you are asked to strike both the open G- and open-high E-strings simultaneously. Then, after a half beat has elapsed, hammer on, with the first finger, to fret 1, string 3 (middle G♯).

Compound Intervals

Intervals larger than an octave are known as *compound intervals*. They are constructed by adding a simple interval (prime through seventh) to an octave. Adding a second to an octave yields a *ninth*; adding a third to an octave yields a *tenth*; adding a fourth to an octave yields an *eleventh*; adding a sixth to an octave yields a *thirteenth*, and so on.

TENTHS

The usefulness of thirds and sixths for fingerstyle was discussed in Chapter 4. *Tenths* are another highly useful interval, made up of an octave plus a third. An octave plus a major third is called a major tenth, while an octave plus a minor third is known as a minor tenth. Whether a given situation calls for a major or minor tenth depends, of course, on the sequence of whole and half steps within the scale you are using. Some major tenths include C-E′, F-A′, A-C♯′, and B♭-D′; some minor tenths are C-E♭′, F-A♭′, A-C′, and B♭-D♭′.

TENTHS AND THE GUITAR

Tenths also form distinct patterns on guitar, as shown in figure 5–8. Observe that for all of these patterns, the two notes that form the tenth are separated by two intervening strings. Major tenths are shown in figure 5–8a. On the low E-G pair of strings, they are all one fret apart; on the A-B and D-high E pairs, they are two frets apart. Figure 5–8b shows minor tenths. These are all one fret apart on the A-B and D-high E pairs and on parallel frets for the low E-G pair. (Observe that the open string pair, low E-G, forms a minor tenth interval in its own right.)

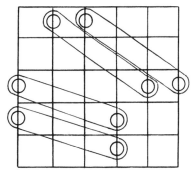

Figure 5–8a

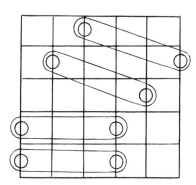

Figure 5–8b

In many instances, a series of melody notes can be beefed up by adding on a corresponding series of "tenth-below" harmony notes. These tenth-below notes then become the bass notes of the passage. When harmonically appropriate, one or more open strings between the two tenth-apart notes can serve as inner voices.

Happy Traum

Happy Traum is one of today's most influential fingerstyle guitarists. His instruction books, which were among the first to appear on fingerpicking, include *Fingerpicking Styles for Guitar, Traditional and Contemporary Fingerpicking*, and *The Guitar of Brownie McGhee*. In the late 1960s, he founded the Homespun Tapes Company of Woodstock, NY, which provides lessons taped by experts in a variety of musical fields to would-be musicians around the world. Among the series he has himself recorded for Homespun are "Fingerpicking Guitar," "Country Blues Guitar," and "Flatpick Country Guitar." He has performed extensively as a solo artist throughout the United States, western Europe, and Japan. Among his numerous albums are:

Relax Your Mind (Kicking Mule)

American Stranger (Kicking Mule)

Bright Morning Stars (Greenhays)

Friends and Neighbors (Vest Pocket)

Happy and Artie Traum: Hard Times in the County (Rounder)

Happy started fingerpicking in the mid-1950s after seeing Tom Paley play one day in Greenwich Village's Washington Square Park. "He was playing 'Railroad Bill' and several other Hobart Smith tunes in the fingerpicking style" writes Happy "and I was very impressed. Before long, I was one of the many young people who were trying to pick Elizabeth Cotten's 'Freight Train' with varying degrees of success.

"In 1958 I started studying blues guitar with Brownie McGhee, who helped my fingerpicking quite a bit and introduced me to finger-picks, which I still use. At about the same time, I discovered the playing of Merle Travis, Mississippi John Hurt, Furry Lewis, Reverend Gary Davis, Blind Lemon Jefferson, and dozens of others who influenced me. Although I have taken my own path, these great players have always been in the back of my mind, setting a high standard."

This version of "Silver City Bound" was arranged by Happy Traum and appears on his *Bright Morning Stars* album.[3] The song was written by the great blues guitarist Leadbelly (his real name was Huddie Ledbetter) as a tribute to his mentor and friend Lemon Jefferson. Leadbelly started his career in Texas as "lead boy" for Jefferson, guiding the blind artist from engagement to engagement. When times were hard, the pair boarded passenger trains and played for contributions. When asked their destination, they would tell the conductor that they were "Silver City bound." Leadbelly went on to become a masterful blues singer and a pioneer of the 12-string guitar whose playing style was known for its powerful bass lines. (See *Leadbelly: Take This Hammer*, on Folkways.)

In the intro. section of this arrangement, Happy plays the melody on the bass strings. "To get a nice jump to it," he writes, "I often alternate between thumb and index finger on the same string." The result is a cross between Leadbelly style and country flatpicking. In the verse section—which features some minor tenths in the first couple of measures—and in the chorus section, Happy plays the melody on the treble strings in a style reminiscent of Mississippi John Hurt.

VERSE

Silver City bound
I'm silver city bound
Well I tell my baby
I'm Silver City bound
Me and Blind Lemon
Gonna ride on down.

CHORUS

Catch me by the hand
Oh, baby
Blind Lemon was a blind
Man (He'd holler)
Catch me by the hand
Oh, baby
Blind Lemon was a blind
Man

Silver City Bound

Standard tuning
Key: D major (blues scale)

♩ = 138

by Leadbelly
arranged by Happy Traum

(continued)

(continued)

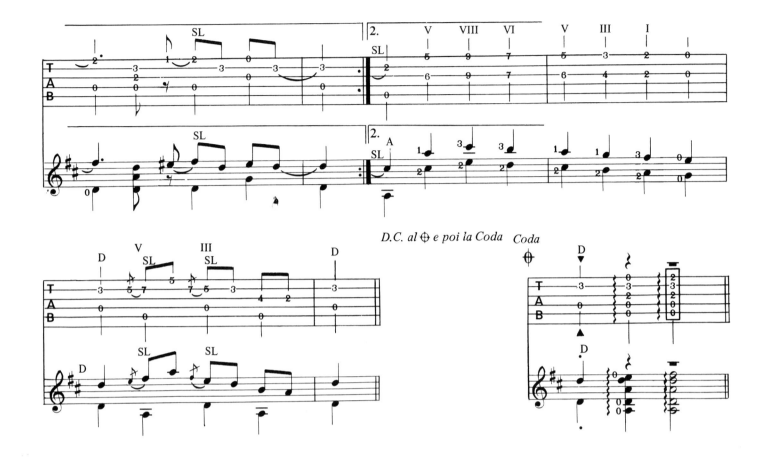

D.C. al ⊕ e poi la Coda   Coda

TECHNIQUE

Brushing the Strings   On numerous occasions in the piece, Happy brushes down on several strings with a simple downstroke of the thumb. This is notated in both tablature and music by a column of notes with *only* a stem originating below the staff. For ease of interpretation, eighth note pairs in which a thumb-played brush is followed by a finger-plucked melody note are shown as two separate single eighth notes. The stem for the brush originates below the staff, while the stem for the finger note originates above the staff. This particular notation appears in measures 3, 9, and 11 of the intro., measure 7 of the verse and measure 7 (first ending) of the chorus.

Sliding with Tenths Intact   In measure 2 of the verse, you are asked to perform two between-beat double slides. Both slides start on a tenth made up of fret 3, string 4 (middle F) and fret 4, string 1 (high A♭). To get the right sound, maintain even pressure and keep the spacing between both fingers intact as you slide up both strings to a tenth made up of fret 4, string 4 (middle F♯) and fret 5, string 1 (high A).

Sliding on One String with a Chord Form Intact   In measures 3 and 7 of the verse and measure 7 of the chorus, you are asked to perform a between-beat slide from fret 1, string 1 (high E♯) to fret 2, string 2 (high F♯). This slide appears in the midst of a passage that should be performed while stopping a basic D chord form. To get this smooth, drop the entire form down one fret (to fret 1) at the start of the slide. Then, maintaining pressure only on the first string, keep the form intact as you slide from fret 1 to fret 2. As soon as you reach fret 2, reapply pressure to all strings in the form.

A Precise Notation for Country Blues

The rhythm for many hard-core country blues tunes is complex and often difficult to notate and read, particularly in conventional $\frac{4}{4}$ time. In the country blues style, the four beats of a measure are each divided into three subbeats or *pulses*, as shown in figure 5–9. You can get a feel for this by tapping out the beats (1-2-3-4) with one hand, while the other hand taps out three pulses per beat *1-2-3, 2-2-3, 3-2-3, 4-2-3*).

Figure 5–9

Beats:	1	-	2	-	3	-	4
Pulses:	1	2 3,	1	2 3,	1	2 3,	1	2 3

Since each beat is routinely composed of three pulses, musical events can (and do) occur on each pulse. This sometimes presents a problem in $\frac{4}{4}$ notation, where it is easy to divide beats by two (eighth notes), four (sixteenth notes), and other multiples of two, but relatively cumbersome to divide beats by three and multiples of three. And while many country blues tunes can be squeezed into $\frac{4}{4}$ time without too much distortion, many of the more complex tunes require a better fitting *meter* (time signature).

$\frac{12}{8}$ Time

$\frac{12}{8}$ time is a meter that, in effect, has four beats per measure, each made up of three subbeats. Figure 5–10 shows two sample $\frac{12}{8}$ measures. Observe that $\frac{12}{8}$ time measures can contain as many as 12

Figure 5–10

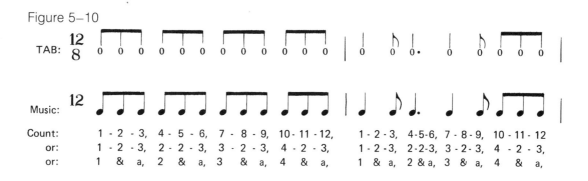

Count:	1 - 2 - 3,	4 - 5 - 6,	7 - 8 - 9,	10 - 11 - 12,	1 - 2 - 3,	4-5-6,	7 - 8 - 9,	10 - 11 - 12
or:	1 - 2 - 3,	2 - 2 - 3,	3 - 2 - 3,	4 - 2 - 3,	1 -2-3,	2-2-3,	3 - 2-3,	4 - 2 - 3,
or:	1 & a,	2 & a,	3 & a,	4 & a,	1 & a,	2 & a,	3 & a,	4 & a,

eighth notes, divided into four groups of three, with an accent falling on the first note of each group. The beginning of each group is considered the "beat," while the individual eighth notes of each group are the pulses. $\frac{12}{8}$ time can be counted in three ways, but the most effective is the last way shown (1-&-a, 2-&-a, 3-&-a, 4-&-a), which most emphasizes the idea of four beats and three pulses.

$\frac{12}{8}$ time is related to both $\frac{6}{8}$ and $\frac{9}{8}$ times, which are discussed at length in *Fingerstyle Guitar* and reviewed in Chapter 6. If you have not yet tried a $\frac{6}{8}$ or $\frac{9}{8}$ piece, I suggest you play through the jig "Tobin's Favourite" (Chapter 6) before proceeding.

$\frac{12}{8}$ VERSUS $\frac{4}{4}$ TIME

$\frac{12}{8}$ notation looks strange at first to those accustomed to reading $\frac{4}{4}$ notation, but the transition is easily made. The basic unit in $\frac{4}{4}$ time is the quarter note, which is counted as 1 beat. In $\frac{12}{8}$ the *dotted quarter note* (equivalent to three eighth notes), *is counted as 1 beat* (see figure 5–10, measure 2). Notes written as eighth-note pairs in $\frac{4}{4}$ time are shown in $\frac{12}{8}$ as quarter note-eighth note combinations. This notation, which implies that the first note of each pair is twice as long as the second note, *reflects the actual way that these notes are played in the country blues style.* (These uneven pairs of notes are known to musicians as *swing eighth notes.*) Notes written as triplets in $\frac{4}{4}$ time are shown in $\frac{12}{8}$ as simple eighth-note groups. Figure 5–11 shows a single measure in both $\frac{4}{4}$ and $\frac{12}{8}$ time.

Figure 5–11

Slapping the Strings

This is a technique used by country blues guitarists for rhythmic punctuation. The plucking hand is angled up so that the thumb curls under a bass string. The bass string is caught with the edge of the thumb, lifted up, and allowed to slap back against the fretboard, yielding a sound resembling a snare-drum beat.

"Big Road Blues" has been recorded by numerous blues guitarists. The opening *motif* (distinctive phrase) in measures 1–3, in which the player vigorously *slaps* all the sixth string bass notes, has become quite famous and has been borrowed for use in other songs by a number of artists, such as Taj Mahal (see *Taj Mahal: The Natch'l Blues* on Columbia). Although you'll have to do some careful counting to get the feel of this motif (see the "Technique" section), the rest of the tune is pretty straightforward and should give you some good practice in reading $\frac{12}{8}$ notation. Observe that for this piece only, the symbol "D♭" stands for an ordinary D-form moved down to the first fret.

Big Road Blues

Tune sixth string to D

Key: D major (blues scale)

♩. = 104

arranged by Ken Perlman

(continued)

TECHNIQUE

Interpreting $\frac{12}{8}$ time   Here's some help getting through the first measure of "Big Road Blues." The idea is to understand exactly what is going on at each "number count" (count 1, count 2. . . .), each "&-count" (first &-count, second &-count . . .) and each "a-count."

pickup note (a-count):	play open 4th string (middle D) with i
measure 1, count 1:	middle D tied over, slap open string 6 (low D) with thumb
first &-count:	both strings continue to sound
first a-count:	play fret 2, string 4 (middle E) with i
count 2:	middle E tied over, slap fret 2, string 6 (low E) with thumb
second &-count:	both strings sound
second a-count:	play fret 3, string 4 (middle F) with i
count 3:	middle F tied over, slap fret 3, string 6 (low F) with thumb. . .

The Stride Bass

The stride bass, sometimes known as double thumbing, is a powerful rhythmic effect used by country blues guitarists. It is most often associated with the playing of Blind Blake (p. 78). The technique was created to imitate the left-hand sound of stride pianists like Jelly Roll Morton (see *Jelly Roll Morton: Piano Classics 1923–4* on Folkways) whose playing represented an intermediate style between classic ragtime (see *Fingerstyle Guitar*) and jazz piano.

In a stride bass, the thumb plucks one string (say string 6) in a downward trajectory and rests heavily on the next higher string (in this case, string 5). The thumb remains in contact with this string, and after a certain period has elapsed, it plucks the string with an upward trajectory. In effect, the thumb plucks two bass strings with one broken movement. The stride bass is notated as shown in figure 5–12, where a slanted line connects two double-thumbed notes. Observe that each stride bass begins on an a-count and that the first stride bass note is an eighth note. The thumb lands on the next higher string, waits for the beginning of the next number count, then plucks that string. At the beginning of figure 5–12, for example, the thumb plucks open low-E on an a-count, and lands on string 5. It waits on string 5 for ⅓ beat, then plucks the open string at the start of count 1. Similarly, the thumb plucks open A on the a-count following count 2, and lands on string 4. It waits on string 4 until the start of count 3, then plucks fret 2, string 4 (middle E), and so on.

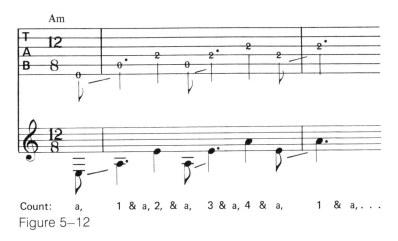

Count: a,   1 & a, 2, & a,   3 & a, 4 & a,   1 & a, . . .

Figure 5–12

THE STRIDE-DRONE BASS

We discussed a one-note-per-beat drone bass in Chapter 4. This technique also appears in $\frac{12}{8}$ time and is notated as shown in figure 5–13a. A more dramatic form of drone bass used frequently in country blues is made up of a series of same-note quarter-eighth combinations, shown in figure 5–13b. This is always *phrased* as shown in the sounds-like segment of figure 5–12b, where each eighth note leads into the following quarter note. Because the overall effect resembles the sound of a stride bass, I call it a *stride-drone bass*.

Figure 5–13a

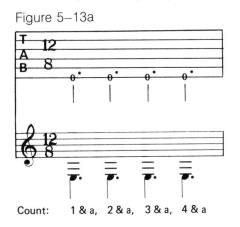

Count: 1 & a, 2 & a, 3 & a, 4 & a

Figure 5–13b

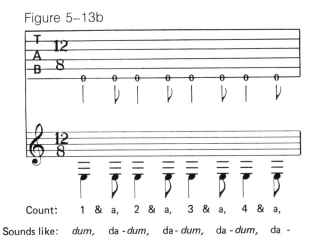

Count: 1 & a,   2 & a,   3 & a,   4 & a,

Sounds like: *dum,* da - *dum,* da - *dum,* da - *dum,* da -

"Hesitation Blues" is another tune that has been recorded by numerous artists. I first learned it in the 1960s from an album called *Dave Van Ronk Sings the Blues* (Verve Folkways), but the best-known version was recorded in the early 1970s by Jorma Kaukonen and his band Hot Tuna. Note the stride bass in measures 1, 2, 3, 8, 11, and 12 of the intro. & verse and in measures 1, 3, 7, 10, and 12 of the break. A stride-drone bass appears in measures 3 and 4 of the break. Remember that any note with an attached stem originating below the staff is played by the thumb, even when it also has an attached stem originating above the staff (see Chapter 2). Special fingering diagrams appear in figure 5–14.

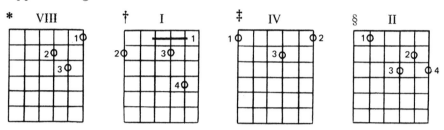

Figure 5–14

VERSE

Well, I'm standin' on the corner
With a dollar in my hand
I'm lookin' for a woman
Who's lookin' for a man
Tell me how long
Must I have to wait
Can I get you now,
Or must I hesitate.

Hesitation Blues

Standard tuning
Key: A minor, C major (blues scale)

♩. = 96

arrangement and break by Ken Perlman

(continued)

D.C. al ⊕ e poi la Coda

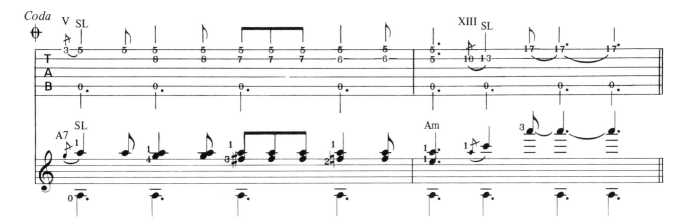

The F♯7 Chord

The F♯7 form is shown in figure 5–15.

Figure 5–15

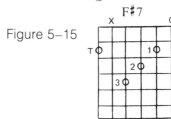

Tonic, Dominant, and Subdominant Chords

The way in which any two chords interact is determined primarily by the distance (interval) between their respective root notes. Chords that are most strongly connected are those in which the root notes are a perfect fifth interval apart (Chapter 4). For example, given any major key, the major triad named for the key is known as the *tonic chord* (C major is the tonic chord of the key of C major, G major is the tonic chord of the key of G major, and so on). The major triad whose root note is a perfect fifth above the root of the tonic is known as the *dominant chord* (G major is the dominant chord of C major, D major is the dominant chord of G major, and so on). The dominant chord tends to lead strongly back to the tonic chord.

The major triad whose root note is a perfect fifth below the root of the tonic is known as the *subdominant* (F is the subdominant of C, C is the subdominant of G, and so on). The subdominant tends to lead either on to the dominant chord or back to the tonic chord. The tonic, subdominant, and dominant chords are not only the most important chords in any major key, but are frequently the only chords you'll need to harmonize a given tune. Figure 5–16 shows tonic, subdominant, and dominant chords for the major keys. Observe that minor seventh intervals are routinely added to dominant major triads, thereby turning them into seventh chords (see Chapter 4). These *dominant seventh chords* have an even greater tendency to lead back to the tonic than do dominant triads.

Figure 5–16	TONIC	DOMINANT	SUB-DOM		TONIC	DOMINANT	SUB-DOM.
	C	G(7)	F		F	C(7)	B♭
	G	D(7)	C		B♭	F(7)	E♭
	D	A(7)	G		E♭	B♭(7)	A♭
	A	E(7)	D		A♭	E♭(7)	D♭
	E	B(7)	A		D♭	A♭(7)	G♭
	B	F♯(7)	E		G♭	D♭(7)	C♭
	F♯	C♯(7)	B		C♭	G♭(7)	F♭
	C♯	G♯(7)	F♯		F♭	C♭(7)	B♭♭

The Circle of Fifths

Because of the nature of the dominant-tonic relationship, a progression of chords can easily be set up that includes every major triad (or dominant seventh chord). One dominant chord (say G) leads to a tonic (C), which itself becomes a dominant chord that leads to another tonic (F), and so on. This series of relationships, known as the *circle of fifths*, is shown in figure 5–17. Knowing how the circle of fifths operates always allows you to find your way back to the tonic, no matter how far away the harmony for a tune might stray. (Observe that the chords listed in parentheses are alternative names for the same groups of pitches.)

Figure 5–17

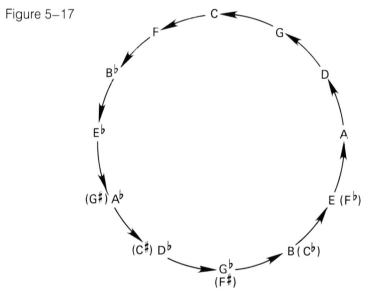

My favorite version of "Trouble in Mind" is performed by Brownie McGhee and Sonny Terry on a record called *Brownie & Sonny* (Everest). The arrangement here features a drone bass, with lots of thirds, sixths, and voice leading thrown in for added color.

Note the circle of fifths progression of chords in measures 5–7 in both the verse and break, which moves from C♯7, to F♯7, to B7, and finally back to E. See figure 5–18 for fingering diagrams.

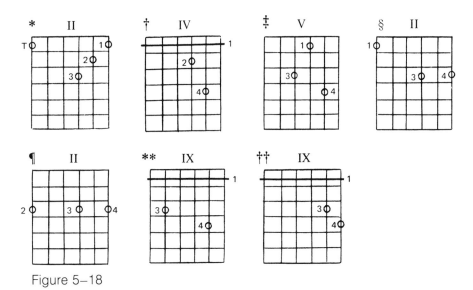

Figure 5–18

LYRICS

Trouble in mind, I'm blue
But I won't be blue always
The sun gone to shine
On my backdoor some day.

Gonna' rock down to the river
In some lonesome easy chair
And if my blues don't leave me
I'll rock on away from there.

Trouble in Mind

Standard tuning
Key: E major (blues scale)

$\quad$ ♩. = 76

arrangement and
break by Ken Perlman

Dealing with Measures
of Different Lengths

Pieces do not always contain the same number of beats in every measure. Sometimes one or even several measures of a tune have either more or fewer beats than the number indicated by the primary time signature. This is notated by placing a new time signature with a different top number at the beginning of these measures. At the conclusion of any short or long measures, the original time signature appears on the staff once again. For example, say the main signature of a tune is $\frac{4}{4}$. If a measure in the piece has only two beats, it is marked with the signature $\frac{2}{4}$; if the measure has three beats, it is marked with the signature $\frac{3}{4}$, and so on. When the tune returns to the original number of beats per measure, a $\frac{4}{4}$ signature appears on the staff.

There are two things to keep in mind when interpreting such passages:

- The first beat of each measure is always accented, *no matter how many beats it contains.*

- *The length of each beat remains constant*, no matter how many occur within a measure.

So if a $\frac{2}{4}$ measure appears in a $\frac{4}{4}$ piece, the count is *1-2-3-4-/1-2-/ 1-2-3-4-/*; if a $\frac{3}{4}$ measure appears in a $\frac{4}{4}$ piece, the count is *1-2-3-4-/ 1-2-3-/1-2-3-4-,* and so on.

Woody Mann

Woody Mann is one of the best-known fingerpickers and guitar teachers of the New York City area. He is noted particularly for his mastery of the country blues idiom, but his playing also includes significant jazz and classical influences. He has done a considerable amount of studio work, accompanying on record such performers as John Fahey (see *Old Fashioned Love,* on Takoma) and Jo-Anne Kelly (see *Jo-Anne Kelly* on Blue Goose). His solo playing appears on two Kicking Mule Records anthologies—*Contemporary Ragtime Guitar* and *Some People Who Play Guitar (Like a Lot of People Don't).* He has recorded a six-tape instruction series called "Fingerstyle Jazz Improvisation," and he has written an instruction book called *Early Blues Guitarists.*

Woody took up the guitar in the early 1960s and had the good fortune to study with both the late great country blues guitarist Reverend Gary Davis and with jazz great Lenny Tristano. A regular performer on the old New York City area coffee house circuit during the late 1960s and early 1970s, he now performs frequently at folk clubs and colleges throughout the United States.

"Cold Feet Blues" is a Woody Mann original.[4] According to Woody, the tune was "inspired by the playing of Lonnie Johnson [see *Mr. Johnson's Blues* on Mamlish] and Charlie Christian [see *Charlie Christian* on Everest], whose styles in many ways overlap. The long legato melodic lines that are a trademark of the two are combined with a rhythmic country blues picking style." Woody mentions that the two numbers that inspired the tune were Johnson's "Hot Fingers" and Christian's "Stompin' at the Savoy."

This tune is fairly difficult and should give your left hand a workout along most of the fingerboard. Part A features a stride bass and swing eighth notes. Part B features a relatively inactive bass (observe all the tied notes) and lots of "triplets" (three-note groupings). Part C is actually a pretty wild jazz-blues break made up substantially of seventh and diminished seventh chord arpeggios interspersed with scale notes and blue notes. "The country blues is a feel rather than a set sound," writes Woody. "The act of improvising on different musical ideas seems to be the central theme of the form." Note that part B, measure 5 is a $\frac{2}{4}$ measure.

[4]"Cold Feet Blues," © 1985 by Woody Mann.

Cold Feet Blues

Tune sixth string to D
Key: D major (blues scale)

♩. = 100

by Woody Mann

"The Mississippi Blues," which was first recorded in the 1920s by bluesman Willie Brown, is one of the best-known instrumental blues pieces of that era.[5] In making this arrangement, I received considerable assistance from Rory Block (p. 78), who had painstakingly worked out many of the exact voicings used on the original recording. (Rory's own version of the tune can be heard on the Kicking Mule album *How to Play Blues Guitar*.) The break, which features a walking stride-drone bass under a series of finger-plucked triplets, is particularly interesting.

The tune is quite difficult both to read and to play. Pay close attention to the rhythm notation, making sure in particular to hold over all tied notes. If not previously evident, the advantages of $\frac{12}{8}$ are certainly obvious in the notation for this tune, which would be impossibly cumbersome to notate in $\frac{4}{4}$ time. Because most of the G-notes in this key-of-A tune are natural, it is considered to be in the A *Mixolydian* mode. This is indicated by a key signature of two sharps (the key of A major has three sharps—see Appendix A). Fingering diagrams for the tune are in figure 5–19.

Figure 5–19

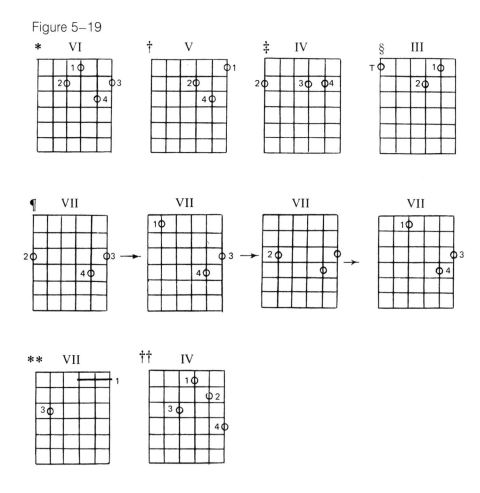

[5]"The Mississippi Blues," arrangement by Rory Block and Ken Perlman, © 1985.

The Mississippi Blues

Standard tuning
Key: A Mixolydian (blues scale)

♩. = 88

Arranged by Rory Block
and Ken Perlman

(continued)

TECHNIQUE

Double Thumbing across an Unplayed String This maneuver appears in measure 3 of the intro. and in measure 11 of both the verse and break. In all three instances, you are asked to play the first stride-bass note on string 6 and the second stride-bass note on string 4. To get the right sound, strike string 6, skip over string 5, and *rest the thumb on string 4*. Then at the proper moment, pluck string 4.

6

Melodic Guitar: Fiddle Tunes and Related Forms

Chapter-opening photos:
left, Gill Burns (photo by Peter Clare);
right, Wendy Grossman (photo by Charles Garvin)

We owe most of our fiddle (folk-dance) *tunes* and ballad melodies to the rural musicians and vocalists of pre-1850 England, Scotland, and Ireland. The music created by these individuals was largely *modal* (that is, nonharmonic) in character. By this I mean that each composer, having little or no notion of what we now call harmony (intervals, triads, and the like), did not take harmonic principles into account when inventing a melody. Only the succession of notes in a particular *mode* (see Appendix A) and the overall sound of the tune were considered important. By contrast, most popular melodies today are composed by putting together a series of chord progressions; they are rarely the product of careful note-by-note choices.

Even though folk-dance and ballad melodies are modal, harmonic principles can be applied to most of them. In other words, there is usually some progression of chords that fits as an accompaniment to each fiddle tune and ballad. The fact that such progressions usually involve just a few simple chords does not mean that these melodies are not complex. It just means that chords are an afterthought when playing modal music.

Modal Music and Fingerstyle

When arranging a modal tune for fingerstyle guitar, the first step is establishing a simple but effective chord progression for the tune. The fewer the chord changes, the more the melody shines through. Then, notes from each chord are used to harmonize (be the bass line or inner voices for) corresponding passages in the tune. Bass notes need not be used on every available occasion—they need appear just frequently enough to establish the harmony and reinforce the tune's basic rhythm.

Tune Categories

Dance-tune categories were discussed at length in *Fingerstyle Guitar*. For the most part, they can be distinguished by time signature. Triple meter tunes ($\frac{6}{8}$, $\frac{9}{8}$, and $\frac{12}{8}$) are in the jig family. Cut time tunes divide, under rather technical grounds into reels, hornpipes, and (in Ireland only) polkas. $\frac{3}{4}$ time tunes such as waltzes and mazurkas are usually intermediate forms between modal music and the formally composed (that is, *classical*) music favored by the aristocracy of the eighteenth and nineteenth centuries.

Vocal melodies (which were until fairly recently performed unaccompanied) partake of a variety of meters, but can be categorized on the basis of theme or function—ballad, work song, drinking song, and so on. A vocal melody played as an instrumental piece is known as a *slow aire*.

Building Triads and Other Chords
from a Scale
(Diatonic Triads and Sevenths)

So far, our discussion of chords has been concerned primarily with instances in which you already know what the harmony is for a given tune. You will often find yourself, however, in situations in which you are faced with a melody and must determine what chords to use with it. This is particularly true of modal music, where chords are not even indicated in most printed sources.

A series of triads can be derived from any major, minor, or modal scale by using scale notes for building blocks. These *diatonic triads* can then be used to harmonize any tune in that key. Using each scale note as a root, we can add to it the scale note that is a third above this root and the scale note that is a fifth above this root. The result is a set of seven triads, one for each note of the scale. Figure 6–1 shows how this process works for the C-major and C-minor scales. The order of whole and half steps within each scale determines whether a given third is major or minor or if a given fifth is perfect or diminished (see figure 4–14). This in turn determines whether a particular triad is major, minor, or diminished.

Diatonic seventh chords can be built by adding to each diatonic

Figure 6–1

C MAJOR SCALE					C MINOR SCALE			
ROOT	3RD	5TH	CHORD		ROOT	3RD	5TH	CHORD
C	E	G	C		C	E♭	G	Cm
D	F	A	Dm		D	F	A♭	D°
E	G	B	Em		E♭	G	B♭	E♭
F	A	C	F		F	A♭	C	Fm
G	B	D	G		G	B♭	D	Gm
A	C	E	Am		A♭	C	E♭	A♭
B	D	F	B°		B♭	D	F	B♭
C′	E′	G′	C		C′	E♭′	G′	Cm

117

Figure 6–2

C MAJOR SCALE

ROOT	3RD	5TH	7TH	CHORD
C	E	G	B	C Maj 7
D	F	A	C	Dm 7
E	G	B	D	Em 7
F	A	C	E	F Maj 7
G	B	D	F	G 7
A	C	E	G	Am 7
B	D	F	A	B° min 7
C′	E′	G′	B′	C Maj 7

C MINOR SCALE

ROOT	3RD	5TH	7TH	CHORD
C	E♭	G	B♭	Cm 7
D	F	A♭	C	D° min 7
E♭	G	B♭	D	E♭ Maj 7
F	A♭	C	E♭	Fm 7
G	B♭	D	F	Gm 7
A♭	C	E♭	G	A♭ Maj 7
B♭	D	F	A♭	B♭ 7
C′	E♭	G′	B♭	Cm 7

triad the scale note that is a seventh above the root note, as shown in figure 6–2. Again, the order of whole and half steps within the scale determines if this seventh interval is major or minor, which in turn determines whether a given chord is a major seventh or just a "plain" seventh chord. Observe that the diatonic diminished seventh chord, which features a minor-seventh interval, is rarely used. The diminished seventh chord used so frequently in blues and ragtime (Chapter 4), which features a diminished seventh interval, does *not* occur diatonically.

MORE ON CHORD RELATIONSHIPS

We've already discussed tonic, subdominant, and dominant chords (Chapter 5). If you look at any scale, the tonic corresponds to the chord built on the first *scale degree* (scale note), the dominant is the chord built on the fifth scale degree, and the subdominant is built on the fourth scale degree. In fact, the tonic is often called the *I-chord*, the dominant is often called the *V-chord*, and the subdominant is often called the *IV-chord*.

The chord built on the third scale degree, which is halfway between tonic (I) and dominant (V), is known as the *mediant* or *III-chord* (Em in the C-major scale, E♭ in the C-minor scale). The chord built on the sixth scale degree, which falls halfway between tonic and subdominant *when the subdominant root note is set a fifth below the tonic root* (see Chapter 5), is known as the *submediant* or *VI-chord* (Am in the C-major scale, A♭ in the C-minor scale). The chord built on the second scale degree is known as the *supertonic* or *II-chord* (Dm in the C-major scale, D° in the C-minor scale), while the chord built on the seventh scale degree is called the *subtonic* or *VII-chord* (B° in the C-major scale, B♭ in the C-minor scale). Frequently, a mediant, submediant, supertonic, or subtonic chord provides a better "fit" for a given portion of a melody than the more commonly used tonic, subdominant, or dominant chords. Figure 6–3 shows triads I through VII for various major and minor keys. Observe that the kind of triad (major, minor, or diminished) is constant from key to key at each major scale degree and each minor scale degree. In other words, the IV-chord in every major key is a major triad, the V-chord in every minor key is a minor triad, and so on.

Figure 6–3

MAJOR KEYS

I	II	III	IV	V	VI	VII
C	Dm	Em	F	G	Am	B°
G	Am	Bm	C	D	Em	F♯°
D	Em	F♯m	G	A	Bm	C♯°
A	Bm	C♯m	D	E	F♯m	G♯°
E	F♯m	G♯m	A	B	C♯m	D♯°
B	C♯m	D♯m	E	F♯	G♯m	A♯°
F♯	G♯m	A♯m	B	C♯	D♯m	E♯°
C♯	D♯m	E♯m	F♯	G♯	A♯m	B♯°
F	Gm	Am	B♭	C	Dm	E°
B♭	Cm	Dm	E♭	F	Gm	A°

MINOR KEYS

I	II	III	IV	V	VI	VII
Cm	D°	E♭	Fm	Gm	A♭	B♭
Gm	A°	B♭	Cm	Dm	E♭	F
Dm	E°	F	Gm	Am	B♭	C
Am	B°	C	Dm	Em	F	G
Em	F♯°	G	Am	Bm	C	D
Bm	C♯°	D	Em	F♯m	G	A
F♯m	G♯°	A	Bm	C♯m	D	E
C♯m	D♯	E	F♯m	G♯m	A	B
Fm	G°	A♭	B♭m	Cm	D♭	E♭
B♭m	C°	D♭	E♭m	Fm	G♭	A♭

119

Gill Burns, a guitarist from Merseyside, England, has performed extensively in Britain, Ireland, and northern Europe. Her playing appears on *The Women's Guitar Workshop* (Kicking Mule), and she has a solo album on No Such Records entitled *Aloan at Last*.

Gill took up the guitar in the early 1970s. "A college friend taught me the chord C and without books or further human help, I proceeded to discover the delights of the guitar fretboard." Some years later she developed an interest in Irish and English fiddle tunes, and after an unsuccessful attempt at learning to fiddle, she began working out ways of adapting the music to fingerstyle guitar.

Lately, Gill has been experimenting with a custom-built seven-string guitar, whose added high-A string (tuned above open high E) allows her to play just about every fiddle tune without leaving first position. She has also become active in the Amsterdam Folk Collective, whose anthology album, *Melange*, includes some of her material.

Gill Burns arranged for guitar "Tobin's Favourite," a well-known Irish jig.[1] Jigs are in $\frac{6}{8}$ time, which means that each measure contains up to six eighth notes. These are divided into two groups of three, counted 1-2-3, 4-5-6; 1-2-3, 2-2-3; or most effectively, 1 & a, 2 & a. A quarter note can be substituted for any two eighth notes, and a dotted quarter note replaces three eighth notes.

Gill's version of this tune, which centers on such basic chord forms as C, F, and G7 shows very clearly the process of how finger-picked fiddle tune arrangements are constructed. Gill's bass line is a direct outgrowth of the alternating bass style. She plays four bass notes per measure. Two of these bass notes are quarter notes and are played along with the *first* note of each eighth note group. The other two bass notes are eighth notes and are played along with the *last* note of each eighth note group. On a few occasions (part A, measures 3, 7, and 8 and part B, measures 3 and 7), one of these bass eighth notes is employed as a melody note. If you've never played a jig before, I suggest that you play through and get a feel for just the melody of this tune before trying to add the bass line. Since the tune is ordinarily played in the key of D Major, you'll have to place a capo at the second fret in order to play along with other instruments.

[1]"Tobin's Favourite," arrangement © 1985 by Gill Burns.

Tobin's Favourite

Standard tuning
Key: C major
(Fiddler plays in D)

♩. = 84

arranged by Gill Burns

Capo-2 with Fiddle

121

Baroque Guitar Tuning (E-A-D-*F♯*-B-E)

Prior to about the middle of the eighteenth century, the third string of the guitar was routinely tuned to F♯ instead of G. This means that the major third interval on the instrument fell between strings 3 and 4 instead of between strings 2 and 3. Tuning the third string to F♯ gives the guitar a slightly different tonality, and of course, means that slightly different fingerings must be used for the various chord forms. To obtain *Baroque tuning* from standard tuning, merely tune string 3 down to match the pitch of fret 4, string 4 (middle F♯). Since the third string is tuned down a half step, standard notation users must remember that all pitches on the string are now *located one fret higher*.

Lynn Clayton

Lynn Clayton is a guitarist and songwriter from Crawley, England. She performs frequently at folk clubs and festivals in southern England and has toured parts of the United States. Her playing appears on *The Women's Guitar Workshop* (Kicking Mule), and her solo album, *Lynn Clayton*, is on Airship Records.

Lynn took up the guitar at the age of nine, having been inspired by a recording of blues singer Big Bill Broonzy (see *Big Bill Broonzy: 1930's Blues* on Biograph). As to others who influenced her playing, she mentions "Don McLean, Paul Simon, Joni Mitchell, and guitarists too numerous to mention around the [English] folk club circuit."

Lynn Clayton learned parts C and D of "Curranta for Mrs. Elizabeth Murcott" from Dick Richardson.[2] These parts were composed during Elizabethan times by Francis Pilkington. (A *curranta* is a slow, elegant dance tune.) Parts A and B were composed by Lynn, who felt that since it was "a very short piece, it seemed a good idea to lengthen it with something of my own." A fingering diagram appears in figure 6–4.

Figure 6–4

2"Curranta for Mrs. Elizabeth Murcott" (parts A and B) by Lynn Clayton, © 1985; arrangement (parts C and D) by Lynn Clayton © 1985.

Curranta for Mrs. Elizabeth Murcott

Tuning: E-A-D-F#-B-E

Key: Parts A, C, and D: E major

Part B: E Dorian

♩ = 100

Parts A and B: by Lynn Clayton

Parts C and D: by Francis Pilkington

(continued)

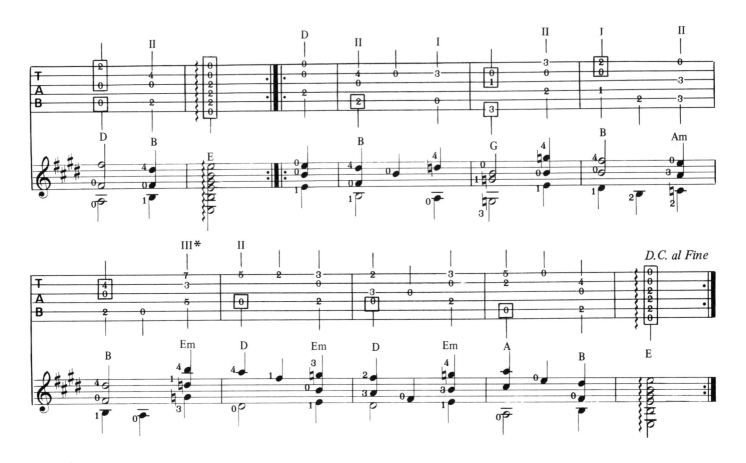

A Hammer-on and Pull-off Warmup

Those of you who have tried some of the fiddle tunes in *Fingerstyle Guitar* or in *Fingerpicking Fiddle Tunes* know just how important strong and even hammer-ons and pull-offs are to the overall effectiveness of a rendition. Over the years, I've gradually perfected a daily warmup routine that progresses gradually from the simplest to the most demanding H and P maneuvers. As you practice this series of exercises, concentrate in particular on refining and improving the efficiency of your movements so that each H and P (or series of H's and P's) is produced with the smallest possible effort.

The entire warmup is in second position, which means that all second fret notes are stopped by the first finger, all third fret notes are stopped by the second finger, all fourth fret notes are stopped by the third finger, and all fifth fret notes are stopped by the fourth finger.

If you have trouble stretching out to perform any of the suggested maneuvers in second position, take the whole exercise up the neck one or more frets until you find a location where they are relatively comfortable. Then, work your way back down to second position at a rate of about one position per month. (If you are initially comfortable in fifth position, stay there for a month, then try fourth position for a month, and so on.) Since the actual pitches played are unimportant, the exercise is presented in tablature only.

Hammer-on and Pull-off Warmup

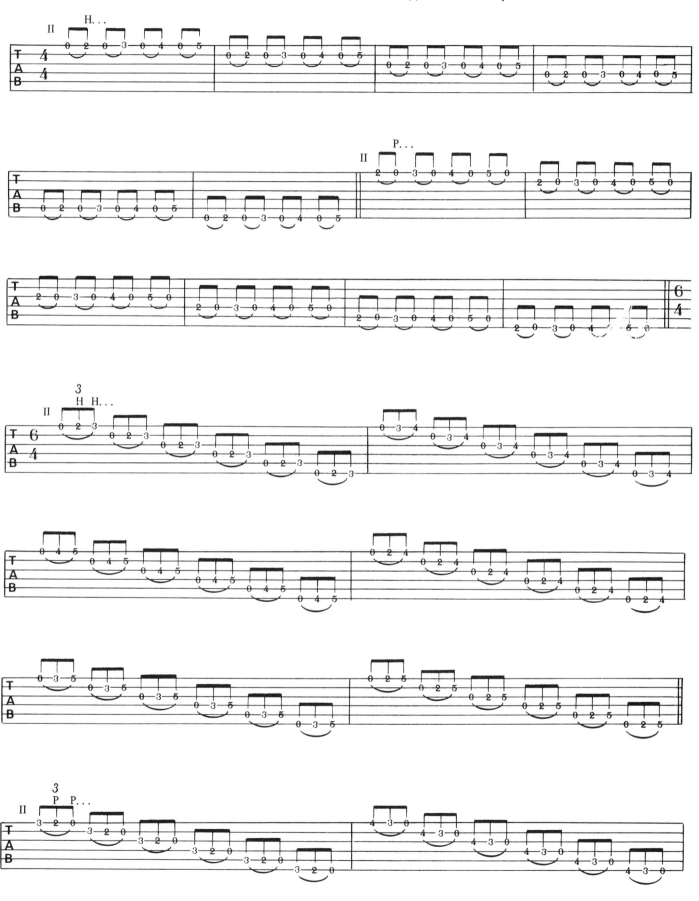

(continued)

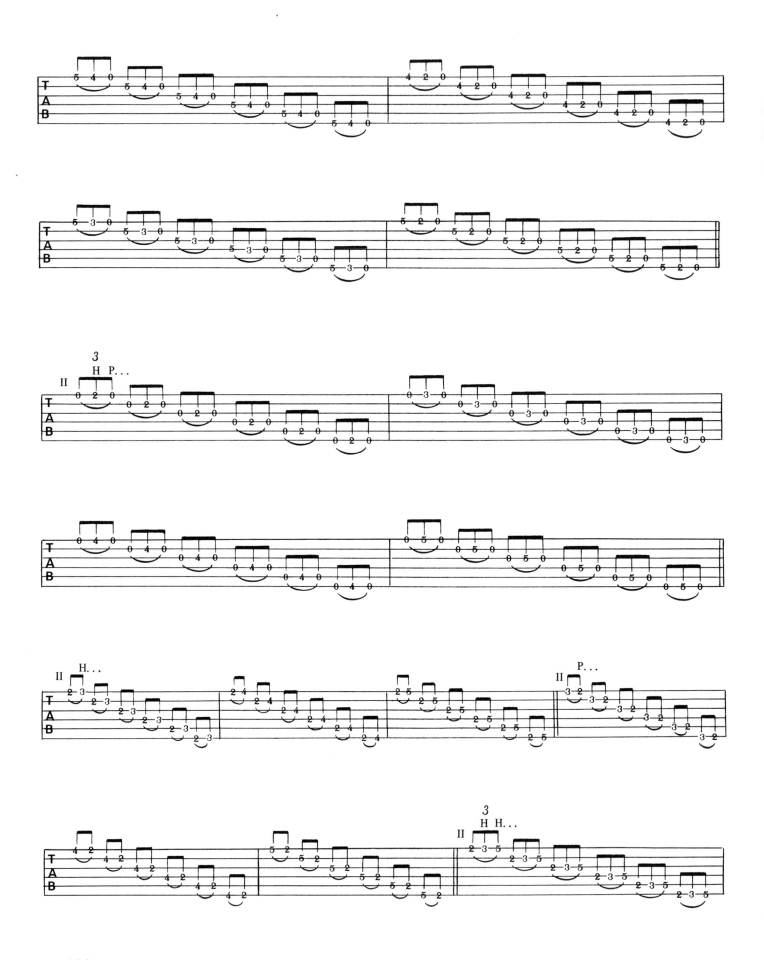

126

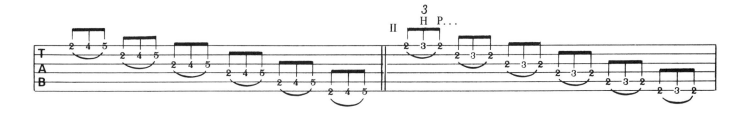

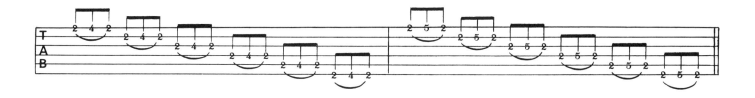

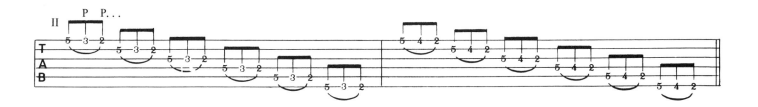

Building Chords from Modal Scales

Diatonic triads and seventh chords can be constructed by applying the same procedure to modal scales (Dorian, Mixolydian, and so on) that was used for major and minor scales (see p. 117). In other words, chords can be built using notes found in the scale on each and every scale degree. The resulting chords are then numbered I through VII, labeled tonic, dominant, mediant, and so on, and used for harmony in the same way as major-key and minor-key chords.

ALTERED SCALES

There is one problem with this approach—namely that the official dominants (that is, the V-chords) of the Dorian, Mixolydian, and Aeolian modes do *not* strongly lead back to their respective tonic chords. The Western ear is accustomed to hearing a major chord in the role of dominant, but the V-chords for all Aeolian, Dorian, and Mixolydian keys are minor traids. To deal with this state of affairs, musicians invented *altered scales* in which the seventh degree is raised a half step.

127

This raised seventh degree has the effect of raising the middle note of the V-chord triad a half step, thereby turning it from a minor to a major triad. This process is most often applied to the Aeolian (natural minor) mode, which when altered in this manner is known as the *harmonic minor* scale. For example, the A-natural minor scale runs A-B-C-D-E-F-G-A and has as its V-chord the triad Em (E-G-B). If the seventh degree of the scale is raised to G♯, the V-chord becomes E major (E-G♯-B). Occasionally, Mixolydian and Dorian scales are also altered in this manner.

MODAL DOMINANT CHORDS

For unaltered Dorian, Aeolian, or Mixolydian scales—such as the ones appearing in many fiddle tunes—the VII-chord (a major triad in all three modes) usually serves the role of dominant. A quick way to determine the VII-chord for any of these scales is to find the major triad whose root is a major second below the tonic note. For example, the VII-chord for D Dorian, D Aeolian, or D Mixolydian tunes is C major; the VII-chord for G Dorian, G Aeolian, or G Mixolydian tunes is F major, and so on.

"Banish Misfortune," a three-part jig, was popularized in the early 1970s by the well-known Irish instrumental group, The Chieftains (see *The Chieftains* #2 on Claddaugh). Since then, the tune's unusual melody and its ability to translate well to a variety of instruments and playing styles have made it one of the most widely recorded fiddle tunes. Since the tune is in the D Mixolydian mode, the triad that serves the role of dominant is the VII-chord (C major). Observe the presence of the C♯ (fret 2, string 2) *accidental* in measure 8 of parts A, B, and C. This temporary *alteration* of the scale appears in a number of Irish D Mixolydian tunes and has the function of leading to the last tonic note of each section with a greater sense of finality. Remember that grace notes are played as pinches with bass notes, even though they are written off to the left of the bass-treble alignment of full-fledged notes (Chapter 3).

I have previously published two other versions of "Banish Misfortune"—one in the *Melodic Clawhammer Banjo* book and one in the April 1979 issue of *Guitar Player* magazine.

Banish Misfortune

Tune sixth string to D
Key: D Mixolydian

$\dot{} = 104$

arranged by Ken Perlman

(continued)

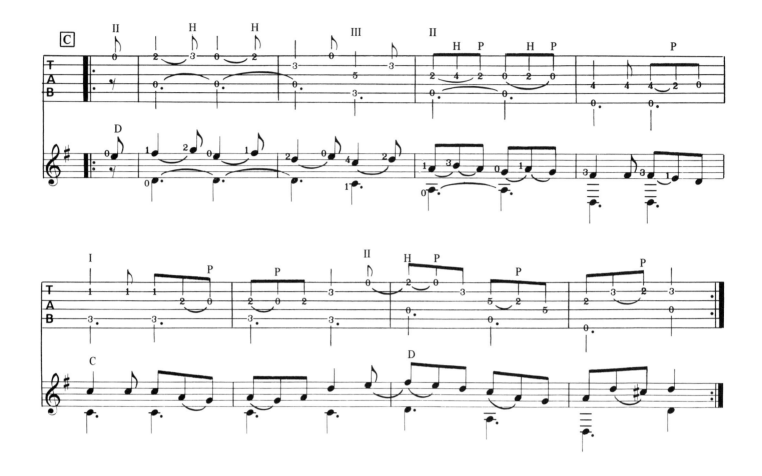

TECHNIQUE

Anchoring H's and P's   In part A, measures 1, 2, 7, and 8, and in parts B and C, measures 7 and 8, there's quite a bit of hammering on and pulling off going on. The fretting hand must be well-balanced to accomplish this smoothly, and one effective balancing method is to "anchor" a finger on a particular string while using other fingers to perform H's and P's on neighboring strings. At the very start of the piece, for example, press down fret 3, string 2 (middle D) with your second finger *before* you start the H-P sequence with the first finger that moves from open string 1, to fret 2, string 1, and back to open string 1 (E-F♯-E). Then, keep anchored on D, and pivot the first and fourth fingers into position to perform a P from fret 5 to fret 2 (C-A), string 3.

"Foxhunter's Jig" is a well-known Irish *slip jig* ($\frac{9}{8}$ time tune). After all those $\frac{12}{8}$ time tunes in Chapter 5, $\frac{9}{8}$ should be a cinch, but I'll review the meter here. Briefly, $\frac{9}{8}$ measures can each contain as many nine eighth notes divided into three groups of three with an accent falling on the first note of each group. The count: 1-2-3, 4-5-6, 7-8-9, or 1-2-3, 2-2-3, 3-2-3, or ideally, 1 & a, 2 & a, 3 & a. I learned this

Foxhunter's Jig

Tune sixth string to D
Key: D major

arranged by Ken Perlman

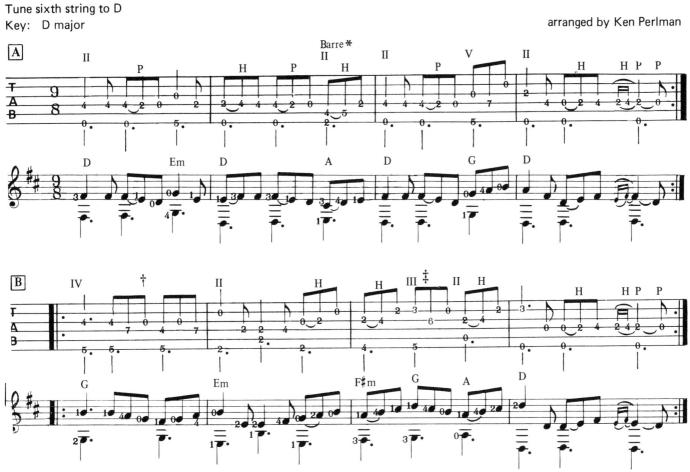

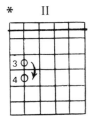

Figure 6–5

tune from Howie Bursen, who plays a fine clawhammer banjo version on his album *Cider in the Kitchen* (Folk Legacy), tablature for which is in *Clawhammer Style Banjo*. Note the harp-effect fingering patterns (Chapter 3) in part B, measures 1 (marked with a dagger) and 3 (marked with a double dagger). Fingering diagrams are in figure 6–5.

"Swingin' on a Gate" is a New England reel. Reels are fast dance tunes in cut time. Cut-time tunes have two beats per measure with half notes counting as one beat. (You'll get the right feel if you read the tune in ⁴₄ time but accent only beats 1 and 3 of each measure.) This particular tune is widely played at New England contra-dances, where it is usually associated with a dance of the same name. During the course of this dance, the tune is repeated endlessly, making it a simple matter for a musician to learn the tune in a single session (this is how I learned it). This arrangement is featured on my Folkways

Swingin' on a Gate

Standard tuning
Key: G major

arranged by Ken Perlman

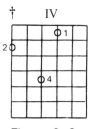 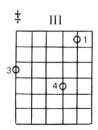 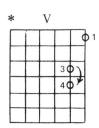 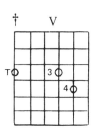 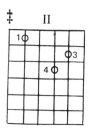

Figure 6–6

album, *Ken Perlman: Clawhammer Banjo and Fingerstyle Guitar Solos*. Fingering diagrams are in figure 6–6.

TECHNIQUE

Playing a Run of Several Notes on a Single String Anytime a run of more than a couple of notes is played on the same string, it is very likely that you will have to shift positions at least once. In part B, measures 1 and 5, you must shift from second to fifth position and back again—all without the benefit of a rest, open string, or even a long note. Playing this passage smoothly requires excellent finger balance. The first shift occurs after an H from fret 3-5 (G-A), string 1. Cut fret 5 short, ride noiselessly (and very quickly) up the string to fifth position and begin your P from fret 7-5 (B-A), string 1. Then cut fret 5 short and ride noiselessly down the string back to second position.

Determining the Harmony for a Tune

An effective harmony for most tunes can be determined by examining the melody notes within it, passage by passage. Each passage in a tune either outlines (spells out) or suggests a particular triad or seventh chord. The simplest case is when a run of melody notes actually spells out the notes of a triad. In part A, measure 1 of "Taylor's Twist," for example, the melody is D-A-F♯-D, A-F♯-D-A, spelling out the triad D major (D-F♯-A), which happens conveniently to be the tonic chord for the key. An intermediate case is when all the notes of a triad are spelled out, but the passage also includes what are known as *passing* or *nonharmonic* tones. The melody of the first half of part A, measure 2 of "Taylor's Twist," for example, is made up of the notes B-G-E-D. Here, the triad G major (G-B-D), the subdominant chord in the key, is spelled out, while E is considered a passing tone.

HARMONIZING AMBIGUOUS PASSAGES

Determining the harmony is most difficult when a passage offers a number of possibilities. The melody might contain only one or two notes, or it may be hard to decide which notes are harmonic and

133

which are passing tones. A good way to start deciphering these situations is to list all diatonic triads and seventh chords for the key along with their "spellings" on a sheet of paper. You can then see at a glance which chords are good possibilities for use in a given situation and which are not.

If a passage is made up of only a single note, this suggests three possible triads. For example, the note C in the key of C major suggests the triads C (C-E-G), F (F-A-C), and Am (A-C-E). Which of these triads you choose for harmony *depends on your ear*. When a passage is made up of two notes, it will probably suggest a couple of triads. For example, the melody line C-E-E-C (in the key of C major) suggests either a C triad (C-E-G) or an Am triad (A-C-E). When a passage is made up of several notes that could suggest a number of triads, *the final decision is made by your ear*.

HINTS FOR CHOOSING CHORDS

The following hints will assist you in determining harmonies.

- For most melodies, the tonic (I-chord) is usually the most frequently occurring chord. It tends to appear at the beginning, middle, and end of a melody.

- The dominant (V-chord, VII-chord for some modal keys) is the second most likely possibility. It tends to appear just before the middle and just before the end of a melody. Observe that V-chords are nondominants in unaltered modal keys; VII-chords are nondominants in major and altered modal keys (see pp. 127–128).

- If the tonic and dominant chords don't work, try the subdominant (IV-chord). If the subdominant doesn't fit, try the II-, III-, VI-, or *nondominant* V- and VII-chords and *choose the one that sounds best to you*.

Looking at the second half of part A, measure 2 of "Taylor's Twist," for example, the melody notes are C♯, B, A, and G. This could suggest a G triad (G-B-D), an Em triad (E-G-B), an F♯m triad (F♯-A-C♯), a C♯° triad (C♯-E-G), or an A triad (A-C♯-E). I felt the best fit was an A, or better yet, an A7 chord (A-C♯-E-G), making B a passing tone.

"Taylor's Twist" is an Irish hornpipe. Hornpipes are cut-time tunes generally played at a slow-to-moderate pace with dotted pairs (figure 2–8) instead of even eighth notes. In practice, the first note (the dotted note) of each dotted pair is actually twice as long as the second note of the pair, even though the notation implies that it is three times as long. (Think of a dotted pair as a triplet in which the first and second notes are tied.) I learned the tune from an album called *Andy McGann and Paddy Reynolds* (Shanachie). This arrangement, which appears on my Folkways album, *Ken Perlman:*

Clawhammer Banjo and Fingerstyle Guitar Solos, is quite difficult and requires substantial practice to achieve the *lilt* so often associated with Irish music. An arrangement of the tune is also in my *Melodic Clawhammer Banjo* book. Fingering diagrams appear in figure 6–7.

Taylor's Twist

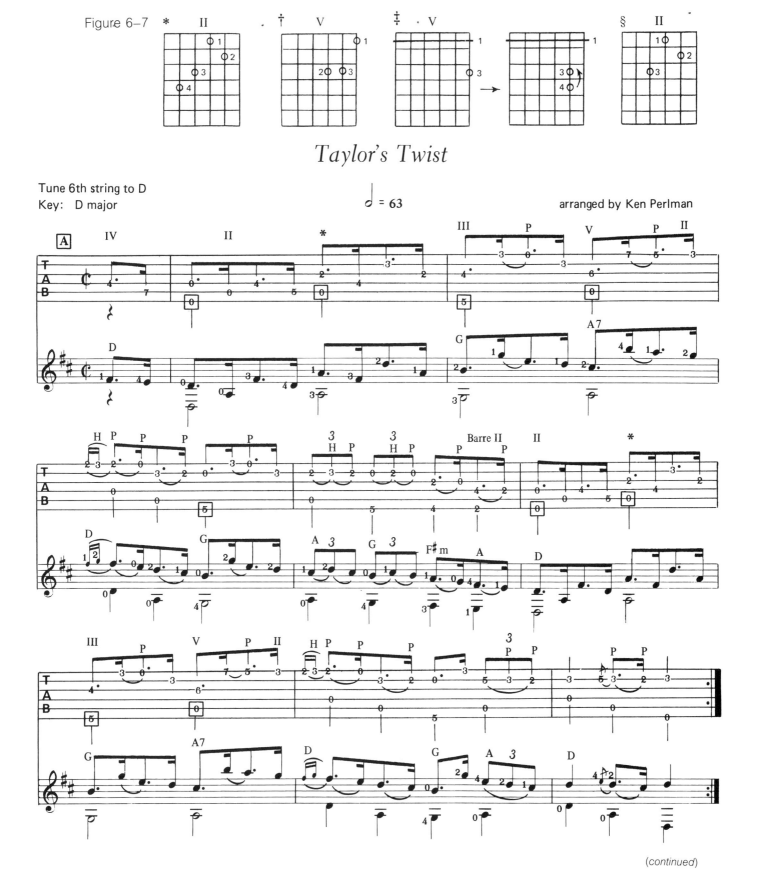

Tune 6th string to D
Key: D major

♩ = 63

arranged by Ken Perlman

(continued)

TECHNIQUE

More on Finger Balance Part A, measure 4 might be one of the hardest passages you'll encounter in this book. Good balance is essential for getting the measure smooth. Start with an H-P triplet on frets 2-3-2 (C#-D-C#), string 2 played over an open A bass. Balance on fret 2, string 2 with your first finger and pivot your hand so that the fourth finger can stop fret 5, string 6 (low G). Hold on to low G and perform an H-P triplet on frets 0-2-0 (B-C#-B), string 2. Then pivot on your fourth finger and get your first and third fingers into position to stop fret 2, string 3 (middle A) and fret 4, string 6 (low F♯). Use the first finger to pull off fret 2, string 3, and balance on the third finger. Then use the third finger as a pivot to get your first finger in position to barre across fret 2 and your fourth finger in position to stop fret 4, string 2 (middle F♯), and so on.

The Scotch Snap

The Scotch snap, so named because of the bowing movement that produces it on fiddle, is a reverse dotted pair in which the sixteenth note is first, as shown in figure 6–8. In a dotted pair, as you know, the first note is in practice twice as long as the second note. In a Scotch snap, the first note is in practice only half as long as the second note. To get the right sound, treat the snap as a triplet in which the second and third notes are tied, count 1 & a, 2 & a, and so on. As figure 6–8 indicates, play the sixteenth note on a number count and the dotted eighth note on an &-count. Allow the dotted eighth to sound through the a-count.

Scotch snaps, as you might expect, are a common feature of Scottish dance tunes, where they mark points that call for energetic leaps. The first note in a Scotch snap is usually accented heavily.

Figure 6–8

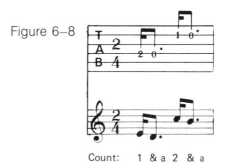

Count: 1 & a 2 & a

Dad-gad Tuning (D-A-D-G-A-D)

A number of prominant guitarists who specialize in British and Irish music have in recent years abandoned standard tuning in favor of what has become known as *Dad-gad* tuning. Dad-gad gives the guitar a beautiful tonality, opens up a number of interesting possibilities for the guitarist, and is considered by some to be superior to standard tuning for playing modal music. To obtain Dad-gad from standard tuning, tune strings 6, 2, and 1 as for open D tuning (see figure 3–24), but leave string 3 at its standard tuning pitch.

137

Wendy Grossman, an American guitarist now living in Ireland, is also a fine vocalist, concertina player, and clawhammer banjo player. She has performed extensively at folk clubs, colleges, and festivals throughout the United States, Canada and western Europe. Her playing is featured on the *Women's Guitar Workshop* (Kicking Mule), and she has appeared as backup instrumentalist on a number of LP's, such as *Archie Fischer: Man with a Rhyme* (Folk Legacy) and *Bill Steele, Chocolate Cookies* (Swallowtail). Her solo album, entitled *Roseville Fair*, is on Lincoln House Records.

Wendy Grossman came up with this arrangement of the Scottish tune "Bonnie Charlie" in Dad-gad tuning.[3] "Bonnie Charlie" was the nickname of deposed monarch James II's grandson, Charles Stuart (1720–88), who led Scottish forces in a vain attempt to retake the British throne. Wendy learned one version of the tune from British folk singer Archie Fischer and another quite different version from a Boys of the Lough album called *Lochabor No More* (Philo). This arrangement takes elements of both versions and transforms the tune into an elegant and unusual guitar piece.

Note the Scotch snaps in part A, measures 4, 5, 13, and 15. Observe also that part A, measure 1 is in $\frac{4}{4}$, but the rest of the arrangement is in $\frac{3}{4}$. The count is 1-2-3-4-/1-2-3-/1-2-3, and so on. The six-string broken chord in part B, measure 3 is obtained by merely brushing all six strings with a downward motion of the thumb. A fingering diagram for the tune appears in figure 6–9. Because so many strings have been retuned, the arrangement is presented in tablature only.

Figure 6–9

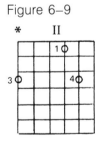

---

[3]"Bonnie Charlie," arrangement by Wendy Grossman, © 1985.

Bonnie Charlie

Tuning: D-A-D-G-A-D
Key: D major

♩ = 92

arranged by Wendy Grossman

TECHNIQUE

Series of Uneven H's and P's from a Single Plucked Note   In parts A and B, measure 16, three notes of unequal time value are obtained via H's and P's from a single plucked note. To get the right sound requires considerable fretting-hand control. Start by plucking fret 2, string 4 (stopped by the first finger). Keep fret 2 sounding for one and a half beats and, without removing the first finger from the fretboard, hammer on to fret 4, string 4 with the third or fourth finger. Since you still have the first finger down on fret 2, it is a simple matter, after a quarter beat has elapsed, to pull off from fret 4 to fret 2. Balance on the first finger at the conclusion of the P, then use it half a beat later to perform an additional P from fret 2 to the open fourth string. Finally, allow open string 4 to sound for a full beat.

In part B, measure 8, go through the same sequence of movements on string 1. Instead of allowing the open-string note to sound for a full beat, however, let only a half beat go by, then perform another H from the open string to fret 2, string 1. Keep fret 2, string 1 sounding for the last half beat of the measure.

"Billy in the Lowground," a well-known Southern fiddle tune, appears in *The Old Time Fiddlers Repertory*. It is closely related to an Irish reel called "The Sailor's Bonnet" (see *The Legacy of Michael Coleman* on Shanachie). This version is based on a 1920s Lowe Stokes recording reissued on *Old Time Fiddle Classics* (County), in which he adds an extra measure to each part. Observe that for Southern fiddle tunes, the notes falling on the second and fourth beats of each measure are accented and that all eighth note pairs are played as *swing eighth notes* (Chapter 5). An arrangement of this tune also appears in *Clawhammer Style Banjo*. See figure 6–10 for fingering diagrams.

Figure 6–10

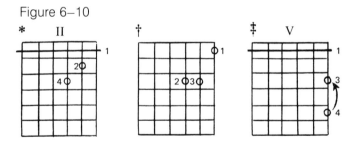

Billy in the Lowground

Tune sixth string to D
Key: D major

♩ = 138

arranged by Ken Perlman

(continued)

MORE H AND P EXERCISES

Here's another series of H and P exercises designed to build up your agility and control. Master each exercise on the first string as shown, then practice it in turn on each of the other five strings. When you are able to perform an exercise smoothly on all six strings in second position, try it in first position, fifth position, or any other position. Since the actual pitches played are unimportant, the exercises are presented in tablature only.

More H and P Exercises

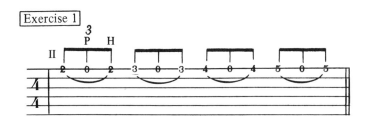

Exercise 1

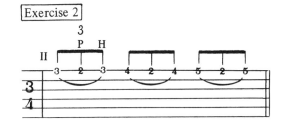

Exercise 2

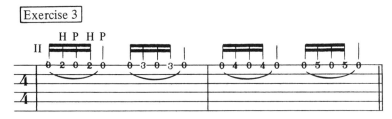

Exercise 3

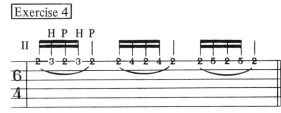

Exercise 4

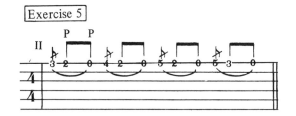

Exercise 5

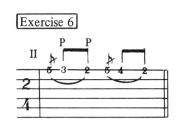

Exercise 6

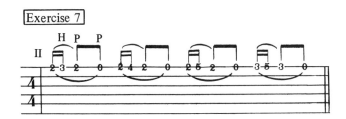

Exercise 7

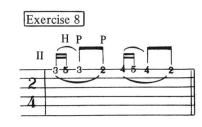

Exercise 8

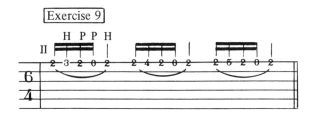

Exercise 9

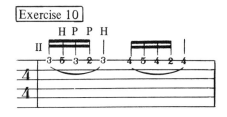

Exercise 10

"O'Carolan's Welcome" was composed by eighteenth century Irish harpist Turlough (rhymes with Sherlock) O'Carolan. O'Carolan was highly influenced by Baroque music and this tune in particular shows a tension between his folk roots and Baroque influences. Part A is highly modal and would make an effective ballad melody. Part B, on the other hand, is distinctly harmonic and contains a number of Baroque clichés. The VII-chord (G major) is used in the role of dominant for both sections. Observe how melodic fingering patterns (Chapter 3) are used constantly to make the guitar mimic the tonality of a harp. I play this arrangement on my album, *Ken Perlman: Clawhammer Banjo and Fingerstyle Guitar Solos* (Folkways). Fingering diagrams are in figure 6–11.

Figure 6–11

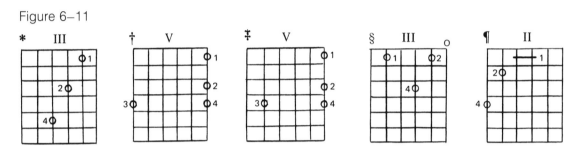

O'Carolan's Welcome

Standard tuning
Key: A Aeolian

♩=100

arranged by Ken Perlman

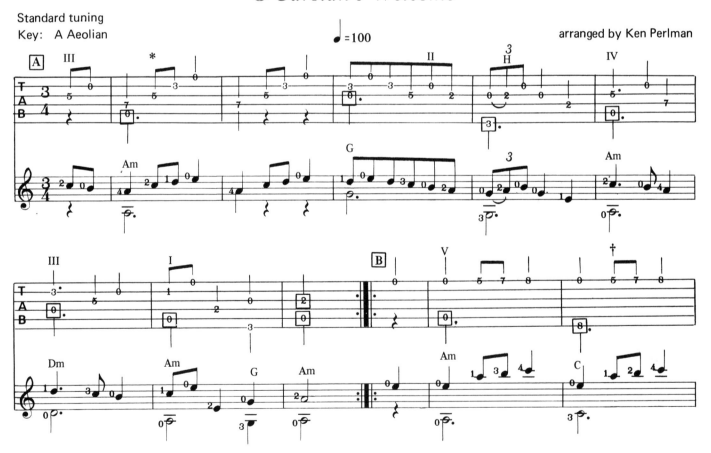

145

7

From Ragtime to Riches: The Frontiers of Fingerstyle

Chapter-opening photos:
left, Glenn Jenks (photo by Cindy La Rock);
right, Pierre Bensusan (photo by Yucky Goldlin)

Before 1650 much of the one-instrument contrapuntal music was composed for guitar and the closely related lute. These instruments had two important drawbacks, however. First, even relatively simple counterpoints required a high degree of musicianship. And, since the fretting hand can only stretch so far, certain combinations of tones were impossible for even the most dexterous and accomplished musicians.

To overcome these problems, *luthiers* (guitar and lute markers) devised what is known as the *baroque lute,* which added several bass strings to the lute's normal complement of five or six strings. These extra strings were played open and formed a descending scale whose pitches could be altered to fit the key of a piece. (The two-necked early twentieth century instrument known as a *harp-guitar* was basically a steel-stringed baroque lute.) As the number of strings increased, however, limitations in the plucking hand's ability to stretch created new difficulties.

The introduction of keyboard-plucked stringed instruments like the virginal, clavichord, and harpsichord in the seventeenth century eventually put an end to this experimentation. On a keyboard, combinations of tones that are impossible on guitar and lute are accessible to virtual novices, and musicians of only modest skills are able to play fairly complex contrapuntal pieces. Before long, composers were writing more solo contrapuntal pieces for keyboards and fewer pieces for guitar and lute. By 1800, both guitar and lute were regarded as quaint anachronisms by the musical establishment.

Since that era, there has not been a great deal of material composed *specifically* for fingerstyle guitar or lute. There is a relatively small body of music by nineteenth and twentieth century Spanish composers, an even smaller body of "new music" for guitar by adventurous present-day classical composers, and a fair number of country blues pieces composed in the 1920s. Most of the fingerstyle pieces now played have been adapted from music composed for other instruments—cello and harpsichord suites, piano rags, fiddle tunes, and so on.

Today, when there are certainly more fingerstyle guitarists than at any time in history, it is not surprising that many players would tire of the standard repertoire and begin to compose their own tunes. Many of the tunes in this chapter, along with some of the original tunes presented earlier in the book, are representative of a new trend among guitarists—an attempt to establish, for the first time since the 1700s, a new literature of guitar pieces and a new approach to the guitar. Instead of trying to make the guitar sound like a cello, harpsichord, piano, harp, fiddle, or other instrument, these composers emphasize in their pieces the particular strengths and unique possibilities offered by the guitar.

Compound Chords

When a compound interval (Chapter 5) is added to a triad or seventh chord, this new entity is known as a *compound chord*. A *ninth chord*, for example, is made when a ninth interval is added to a triad or seventh chord; an *eleventh chord* is made when an eleventh interval is added to a triad, seventh, or ninth chord; a *thirteenth chord* is made when a thirteenth interval is added to a triad, seventh, ninth, or eleventh chord.

NINTH CHORDS

When musicians use the term *ninth chord*, they are usually referring to a specific chord composed of a seventh chord (that is, a triad plus *minor seventh*) with an added major ninth interval. Chords in which a major ninth interval is added to a major seventh chord are called *major ninth chords*. Ninth and major ninth chords are made up of four adjacent thirds. Some ninth chords are C9 (C-E-G-B♭-D), G9 (G-B-D-F♯-A), and Bm9 (B-D-F♯-A-C♯). Some major ninth chords are CMaj9 (C-E-G-B-D), GMaj9 (G-B-D-F♯-A), and BmMaj9 (B-D-F♯-A♯-C♯).

ELEVENTH CHORDS

When musicians use the term *eleventh chord*, they are referring to a ninth chord (as just defined) with an added perfect eleventh interval. When a perfect eleventh is added to a major ninth chord, it yields a *major eleventh chord*. Eleventh and major eleventh chords are composed of five adjacent thirds. Some examples are C11 (C-E-G-B♭-D-F) and Gm11 (G-B♭-D-F-A-C); CMaj11 (C-E-G-B-D-F), and GmMaj11 (G-B♭-D-F♯-A-C).

THIRTEENTH CHORDS

When musicians use the term *thirteenth chord*, they are referring to a major thirteenth interval added to an eleventh chord (as just defined). A major thirteenth interval added to a major eleventh chord yields a *major thirteenth chord*. Thirteenth and major thirteenth chords are composed of six adjacent thirds. Some examples are C13 (C-E-G-B♭-D-F-A), Gm13 (G-B♭-D-F-A-C-E), CMaj13 (C-E-G-B-D-F-A), and GmMaj13 (G-B♭-D-F♯-A-C-E).

Quite often, one or more notes in a seventh or compound chord are *altered* (raised or lowered one half step) to assist in voice leading or better fit the melody of a tune. This is indicated by adding on to a chord name the particular interval (fifth, seventh, ninth, and so on) that is changed plus a notation to show exactly what is being done to that interval. If an interval is raised a half step, it is proceeded by a "+" or "♯"; if the interval is lowered a half step, it is proceeded by a "−" or "♭". For example, C13♭5+9 indicates a C13 chord with a flatted fifth and a sharped ninth (C-E-G♭-B♭-D♯-F-A), Gm11♭9 indicates a Gm11 chord with a flatted ninth (G-B♭-D-F-A♭-C), and so on.

COMPOUND CHORDS, ALTERED CHORDS, AND THE GUITAR

Compound and altered chords are a harmonizer's dream. With so many notes to choose from and the possibility of altering just about any note to suit a given situation, it is a relatively simple matter to effect multiple voice-leading from chord to chord. For example, moving from the dominant triad G (G-B-D) to its tonic triad C (C-E-G) offers only one opportunity for voice leading—moving a half step from the B-note in the G triad to the C-note in the C triad. Moving from G7♭9 (G-B-D-F-A♭) to C11♯9 (C-E-G-B♭-D♯-F), however, offers several opportunities for voice leading—B to C *or* B♭, D to D♯, F to E, and A♭ to G.

In addition, some notes (in this case G and F) can be held over from chord to chord during the change, creating interesting *suspensions*. The overall effect gives the guitar a very rich and interesting tonality. In fact, there is a whole school of guitar playing known as *chord-melody style*, in which tunes are arranged largely as a series of compound and altered chords. The melody note is played as the top voice of each chord, while the bass line and inner voices progress as much as possible from one to another by way of voice leading and suspensions.

Since a guitarist has available only four fingers and six strings, many compound and altered forms do not include the entire chord, but focus instead on strategic notes. In other words, most of the altered and compound forms you'll encounter are *partial chords* (see Chapters 3 and 4).

The Reprise

When an entire section is repeated in the midst of a long piece of music, it is known as a *reprise*. In the interest of squeezing into the book as many tunes as possible, reprised sections are not reprinted.

Instead, directions appear in the staff such as "Reprise part A," "Reprise part C," and so on. Unless you are instructed otherwise by the text, play the reprised section through only once.

The Vibrato Choke

In a vibrato choke, the duration of a choked note is increased by using the choking finger to rapidly move the string back and forth along the surface of the fingerboard. Start a vibrato choke like an ordinary choke, by pushing the string outward along the fretboard surface. Then quickly reverse directions and pull the string in, reverse directions again and push the string out, and so on. Continue this process for the entire time value of the note. The vibrato choke is primarily an electric guitar technique but it is used from time to time by acoustic players. It is notated by placing a zig-zag line above a "ch" sign, as shown in part B, measure 1 of "Tracy's Rag."

Michael Soloway

Michael Soloway is a classical guitarist, teacher, and composer from Brooklyn, NY, who has performed at a number of classic guitar societies, concert halls, colleges, and folk clubs throughout the northeastern United States. In 1981, his formal debut concert at Carnegie Recital Hall was highly praised by *The New York Times*.

Michael took up classical guitar at the age of nine. He studied subsequently with Leonard Gitano, Stanley Solow, Aaron Shearer, and Manuel Barrueco, receiving a Bachelor of Music degree in guitar from Manhattan School of Music. Some years ago, he became intrigued with the music of Scott Joplin and other ragtime composers and transcribed a number of their tunes for guitar. In fact, his performance at his debut concert of Joplin's *Solace* was singled out for its ability "to bring technique and musicality most perfectly into balance." He has also composed a number of original rags for guitar, some of which appear on his album. He teaches classical guitar at New York University and the Third Street Music School.

"Tracy's Rag" is a ragtime-style piece by Michael Soloway.[1] Classic rags have a standard format of four repeated 16-measure parts (A, B, C, and D), with a reprise of part A falling between parts B and C. This piece has four eight-measure parts, with a reprise of part B falling between parts C and D. (Note that part B *is* repeated during the reprise for this piece.) (Text continued on p. 155.)

[1]"Tracy's Rag," © 1980 by Michael Soloway.

Tracy's Rag

Standard tuning
Key: G major

♩ = 52

by Michael Soloway

152

(continued)

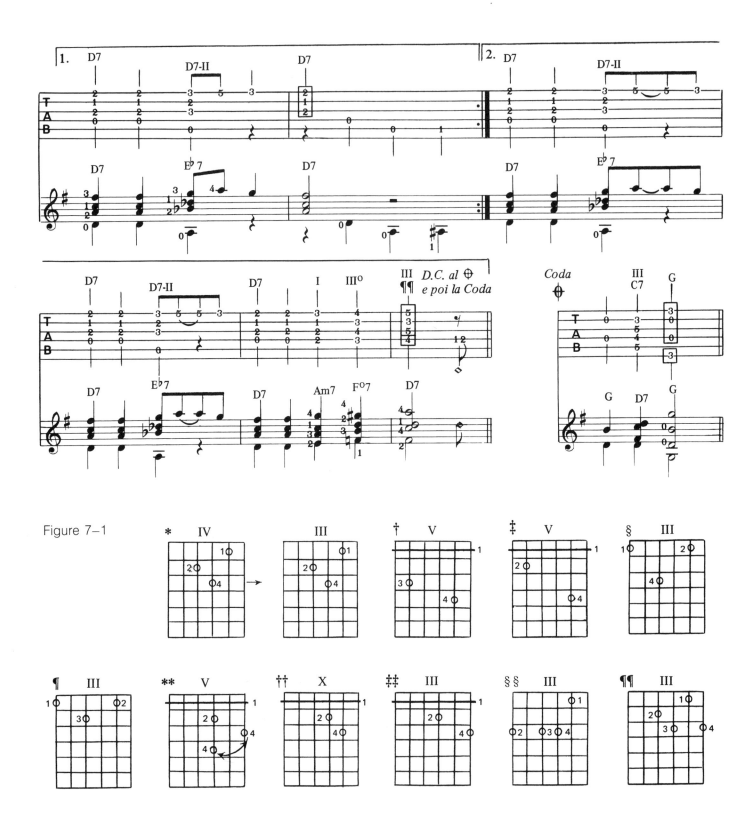

Figure 7–1

Observe how altered chords are used in part C, measures 2 and 5 to add texture and interest to the part; observe also the small *chord-melody* sections in part C, measures 7 and 8, and in part D, second ending, measures 3 and 4. Note also the vibrato chokes in part B, measures 1 and 3. Fingering diagrams for the piece are in figure 7–1.

Pierre Bensusan

Pierre Bensusan of Paris, France, is certainly one of the most dynamic and innovative fingerstyle guitarists and guitar composers of our time. His first album, *Près de Paris* (Rounder), released in 1975 when he was just 17 years old, won the 1976 Montreux Festival Grand Prix du Disque and established him as a master of the fingerpicked fiddle tune. In fact, his version on that album of the Irish jig "Merrily Kiss the Quaker" is now considered a classic of the style. He has since recorded three other albums on the Rounder label devoted primarily to his original guitar compositions. These albums are *Solilai* (winner of an "Honorable Mention" at the 1983 NAIRD Awards), *Musiques*, and *Pierre Bensusan #2*. He tours extensively throughout western Europe, Canada, and the United States.

Pierre was born in Oran, Algeria, and moved with his family to Paris at the age of four, taking up the guitar at age 11. Some of the players whose recordings served as an early inspiration are guitarists Bert Jansch, Davey Graham, John Renbourne, and Martin Carthy of Great Britain, and Eric Shoenberg, Stefan Grossman, and Ry Cooder of the United States. Since early in his career, he has been intrigued by open tunings and he now uses Dad-gad tuning (Chapter 6) almost exclusively for playing and composing. "I found," he writes, "that in order to have a better mastery of guitar playing and a better ability to express myself musically, I needed to concentrate on a single tuning instead of switching back and forth between several tunings."

Pierre finds Dad-gad ideal not only for fiddle tunes and other forms of modal music, but also for fingerstyle jazz, chord-melody, classical guitar, and other styles usually played exclusively in standard tuning. He is at work on a book devoted to original arrangements and compositions in Dad-gad tuning, entitled *Le Livre de Guitare de Pierre Bensusan* (Pierre Bensusan's Guitar Book).

"Le Voyage Pour L'Irlande" (Trip to Ireland), a composition in Dad-gad tuning by Pierre Bensusan, appears on his *Musiques* album.[2] The tune is highly influenced by Irish dance music, borrowing a general modal feel and a two-part eight measure format. The actual melody and rhythmic style, however, is quite original and not derivative of any particular dance-tune form. Note how he drives the tune

[2]"Le Voyage Pour L'Irlande," © 1979 Cezame Productions Editions. Used by special permission of Pierre Bensusan.

Le Voyage Pour L'Irlande

Tuning: D-A-D-G-A-D
Key: D Aeolian

♩= 58

by Pierre Bensusan

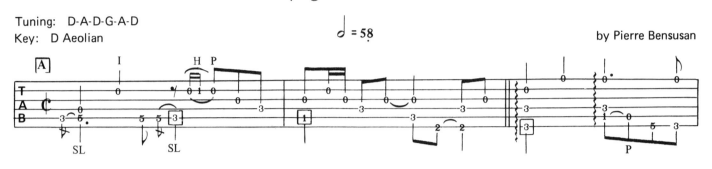

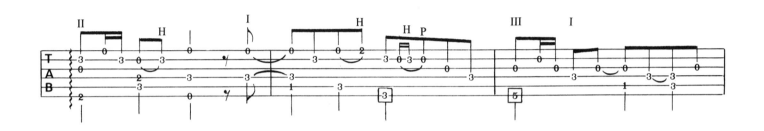

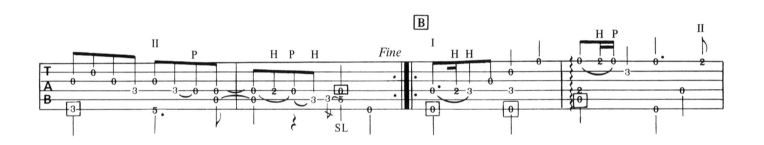

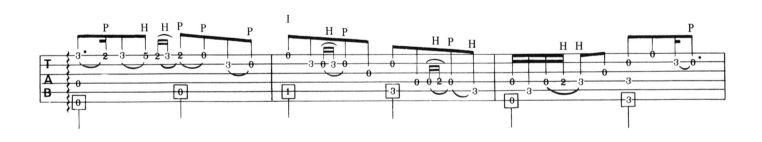

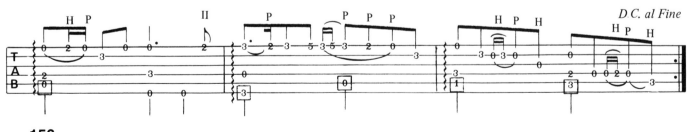

156

156

along by varying the rhythm in general and the location of ornaments (grace notes) in particular from measure to measure. The dominant triad for the tune, which is in the key of D Aeolian, is C major. Since it is in an open tuning, only a tablature version is presented.

Accidentals, the Circle of Fifths, and Harmony Determination

Accidentals (sharps and flats not in the key signature) do not always have harmonic significance. In a melody line, accidentals may just be passing tones (Chapter 6) or blue notes (Chapter 4). For the inner voices or bass line, they may merely be altered tones inserted into the harmony for voice leading purposes. Quite often, however, an accidental in any voice is a sign that you must look beyond the diatonic chords for a particular key (see figure 6–3) to find the proper harmony.

DOMINANT-OF-DOMINANT CHORDS

One place to look for additional chords is the circle of fifths (figure 5–17). In the circle of fifths, a given *dominant* triad or seventh chord (say G or G7) leads to a tonic chord (C or C7), which takes on the role of dominant and leads to a new tonic (F or F7), and so on. Reversing perspective, each *tonic* triad or seventh chord (say F or F7), has a dominant chord (C or C7), which can take on the role of tonic and have its own dominant chord (G or G7), and so on. In other words, the dominant chord of every key has its own dominant, known as the *dominant-of-dominant* or *double dominant* chord. The root note of the double dominant is a perfect fifth above the root note of the original dominant. For example, the dominant of C (or C7) is G (or G7), and the double dominant is D (or D7); the dominant of A (or A7) is E (or E7), and the double dominant is B (or B7), and so on.

Similarly, the double dominant has its own dominant—called the *triple dominant*—which has a root note a perfect fifth above the root of the double dominant; the triple dominant has its own dominant—called the *quadruple dominant*—which has a root note a perfect fifth above the root of the triple dominant, and so on. So if the double dominant of C (or C7) is D (D7), the triple dominant is A (or A7) and the quadruple dominant is E (or E7); if the double dominant of A (or A7) is B (or B7), the triple dominant is F♯ (or F♯7) and the quadruple dominant is C♯ (or C♯7).

When an accidental serves a harmonic role in a piece, it is very likely to be the third of one of these dominant-of-dominant triad or seventh chords. For example, an F♯ accidental indicates a D major triad or seventh chord (D-F♯-A or D-F♯-A-C), a C♯ accidental indi-

157

cates an A major triad (A-C♯-E or A-C♯-E-G), an E♮ accidental indicates a C major triad (C-*E*-G or C-*E*-G-B♭), and so on. The spellings for most major triads appear in figure 4–18; spellings for most seventh chords are found in figure 5–4.

DOMINANTS OF OTHER DIATONIC CHORDS

Not only do tonics (I-chords) and dominants (V-chords) have dominants—but so do II-chords, III-chords, IV-chords, VI-chords, and VII-chords. The dominant for each chord is the major triad or seventh chord whose root note is a perfect fifth above the root of the original chord. These dominants, as it turns out, coincide with many of the dominant-of-dominant chords for that key. In the key of C, for example (see figure 6–1), the dominant of the II-chord (Dm) is the triple dominant chord A (or A7); the dominant of the VI-chord (Am) is the quadruple dominant E (or E7); the dominant of the III-chord (Em), is the quintuple dominant B (or B7), and so on. Put another way, A7 can lead to D7 or Dm, E7 can lead to A7 or Am, B7 can lead to E7 or Em, and so on.

OTHER HARMONIC ACCIDENTALS

Here are some other commonly occurring harmonic accidentals.

Raised or Lowered Thirds   From time to time, a diatonic major triad or seventh chord is changed to a minor triad by lowering the third of the chord a half step, indicated by an appropriate accidental. Similarly, a minor triad can be turned to a major triad by a raised accidental third.

Altered minor scales   When the seventh tone of a minor scale is raised a half step, three triads are affected. The V-chord, as you know (Chapter 6), becomes a major triad, the VII-chord becomes a diminished triad, and the III-chord, which now has a raised or augmented fifth, becomes an *augmented* triad (see p. 168). In an altered A minor scale, for example, the V-chord is E major (E-G♯-B), the VII-chord is G♯° (G♯-B-D), and the III-chord is C augmented (C-E-G♯).

Tonic and Subdominant Seventh Chords   For major keys, the seventh chords built diatonically on the first (tonic) and fourth (subdominant) degrees of the scale are both major seventh chords (see figure 6–2). By lowering the seventh interval one half step, these major seventh chords are turned into "plain" seventh chords. For example, the tonic seventh chord for the key of C major is CMaj7 (C-E-G-B). A B♭ accidental makes the chord C7 (C-E-G-B♭). This C7 chord now serves as the dominant of the IV-chord, F.

Diminished Seventh Chords Diminished seventh chords appear when a seventh chord is built on the seventh degree of a harmonic minor scale (Chapter 6). They resemble ordinary seventh chords in their sound and overall structure and are sometimes substituted for them—particularly in dominant-of-dominant situations. For example, F♯°7 (F♯-A-C-E♭) has pitches virtually identical to those found in D7 (D-F♯-A-C) and is often played in its stead. C♯°7 (C♯-E-G-B♭) closely resembles A7 (A-C♯-E-G) and is often played in its stead, and so on.

The presence of a diminished seventh chord is often tipped off by a pair of accidentals—the third of the closely related seventh chord and the raised root note of that seventh chord. For example, an F♯°7 chord is indicated by an F♯ accidental (which implies a D7) plus an E♭ accidental. When, as is sometimes the case, the raised root of the related seventh chord is already in the key, only a single accidental appears.

Diminished seventh chords have an interesting property. Each diminished seventh chord is composed of three minor thirds. If you take the root note of one of these chords, say F♯°7 (F♯-A-C-E♭), and move it up an octave, you still have a chord made up of three minor thirds (A-C-E♭-G♭[F♯]). This new chord is now called A°7 and is related to F7 (F-A-C-E♭). If you now move the new root up an octave you *still* have a chord made up of three minor thirds called C°7 (C-E♭-G♭-B♭♭[A]), related to A♭7 (A♭-C-E♭-G♭), and so on. In other words, each diminished seventh chord is actually four chords in one.

Glenn Jenks

Glenn Jenks of Camden, ME, is a fine guitarist, clawhammer banjo player, vocalist, and songwriter. He is also one of today's best ragtime piano players. He performs at pubs, festivals, and folk clubs throughout the state of Maine, occasionally venturing forth to do concerts in southern New England and other locations in the northeastern United States. His albums include *Antidote* and *The Ragtime Project* (both on Bonnie Banks) and *Background Music* (Fretless).

Glenn started playing piano at the age of four and studied classical music for 12 years. He took up the guitar in high school. At first, he saw the instrument as a means to escape the intense discipline of his piano studies, but he was soon devoting considerable energy to it. By the time he finished college, he was composing songs and instrumentals on guitar and using it as his major performing vehicle.

In the early 70s, Glenn discovered ragtime piano. He tried to adapt some rags to guitar, found the task unrewarding, and decided to compose some rags of his own for the instrument. He now has a number of fine guitar rags to his credit.

"Hot Chestnuts" is an original guitar rag by Glenn Jenks, appearing on his *Antidote* album.[3] The tune is a classic rag in structure with four 16-measure parts played in the order AA, BB, A, CC, DD. As is customary for the genre, part C is in different key from the other three parts. A four measure bridge between parts C and D brings the tune back to the original key. Observe how an F♯ accidental indicates a D7 harmony in part A, measure 15, part B, measure 15, part C, measure 14, and measure 3 of the bridge; how a C♯ accidental indicates an A7 harmony in part B, the pickup measure and measure 8 and in part D, measures 9, 11, and 12; and how a G♯ accidental indicates an E7 harmony in part A, measure 11 and in part C, measure 13.

Observe also how a B♭ accidental creates the tonic seventh chord C7 in part A, measure 4, part B, measure 12, part A (reprise), measure 16, and in measure 2 of the coda; and how two accidentals (F♯ and E♭) indicate an F♯°7 chord in part A, measure 13, part B, measures 4 and 13, and in part D, measure 12. Fingering diagrams are in figure 7–2.

Figure 7–2

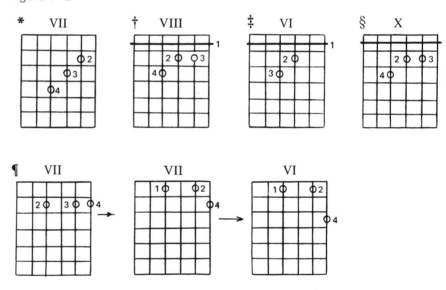

[3]"Hot Chestnuts," © 1978 by Glenn Jenks.

Hot Chestnuts

Standard tuning
Keys: Parts A, B, and D: C major
       Part C: F major

$\downarrow$ = 72

by Glenn Jenks

(continued)

(continued)

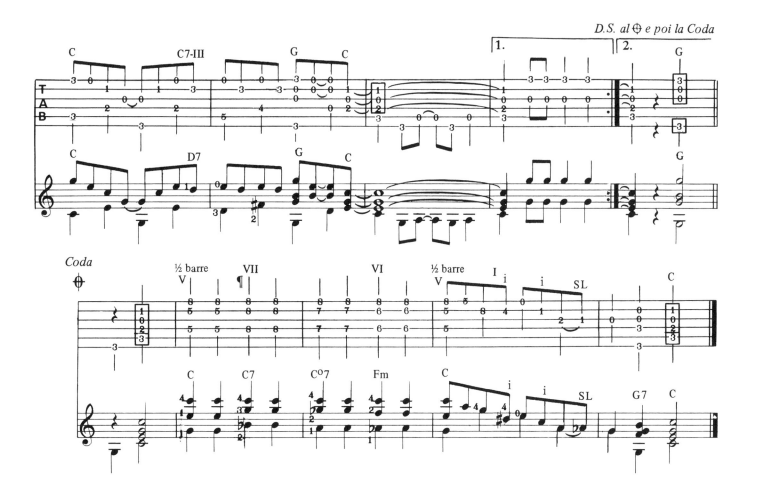

TECHNIQUE

Runs of Same-String Plucked Treble Notes In part B, measures 2 and 10, there is a run of five plucked eighth notes, all of which occur on the second string. To accomplish this, you can either pluck all the notes with the same finger, or for extra smoothness, try *alternating* plucking hand fingers. For practice in this technique, see the Segovia scale study book discussed in Appendix B.

Finger-Stretching Exercises

If you've never played pieces like these before, you may be wondering how your fingers will ever stretch out far enough to reach some of the indicated positions. Here's two simple finger-stretching exercises to help you in this regard. Since the actual pitches played in these exercises are of no consequence, they are presented in tablature only.

Most of the stretch you can acquire is between the first and second and the third and fourth fingers. Exercise 1 works on the stretch between the third and fourth fingers. Starting in seventh position, play fret 7, string 6 with the first finger, fret 8 with the second finger, fret 9 with the third finger, but then *stretch up and play fret 11 with the fourth finger*. Then, hold onto fret 11, string 6, and *stretch up with the first finger* to stop fret 7, string 5. Release the fourth finger and proceed up string 5 in the same manner, stretching from fret 11, string 5 to fret 7, string 4, and so on. On the way down, hold onto fret 7, string 1 with the first finger and stretch with the fourth finger to fret 11, string 2, and so on.

Exercise 2 works on the stretch between the first and second fingers. Stop fret 7, string 6 with the first finger, then stretch to play fret 9 with the second finger, fret 10 with the third finger, and fret 11 with the fourth finger. Then proceed as in exercise 1.

When you become comfortable with these exercises in seventh position, take them down a fret to sixth position. When sixth position is no longer a challenge, take them down to fifth position, and so on. Eventually, you should be able to perform these exercises in second and first positions, which will enable you to handle most of the stretches you'll encounter. Expect the entire process of acquiring stretch to take *at least several months*. Be aware that attempting long stretches before you are ready can cause damage to your hand. For additional stretching practice, see the Segovia and Leavitt scale studies discussed in Appendix B.

Finger-Stretching Exercises

Exercise 1

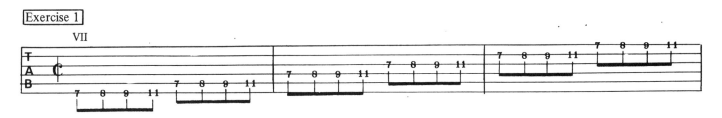

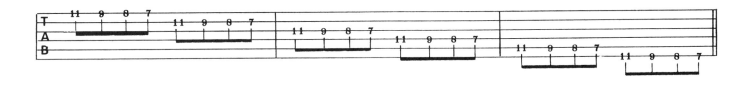

Exercise 2

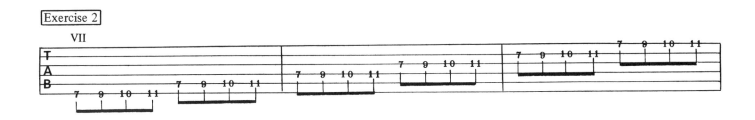

Augmented Chords (Symbol: +)

Augmented chords, which appear routinely as the III-chords of altered minor scales (see p. 158), are triads in which the fifth is raised or *augmented* a half step. They are composed of two major thirds sharing a middle note. A C+(augmented) chord is C-E-G♯; a G+ chord is G-B-D♯; and E+ chord is E-G♯-B♯, and so on. Augmented seventh chords (notation: C7+, G7+, E7+) are "plain" seventh chords with an augmented fifth. Both augmented and augmented seventh chords can substitute in some situations for dominant seventh chords with the same root. They have a distinctive sound and often appear in jazz and show tunes. Both barre and nonbarre standard forms for "+" and "7+" chords are shown in figure 7–3. The notation above the tablature staff for an augmented chord is a barre sign and/or Roman numeral with a "+" or "7+" suffix. An indication above the standard notation staff shows the actual pitch of the chord.

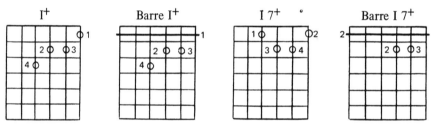

Figure 7–3

Augmented chords have a property similar to diminished seventh chords. If you take the root note of an augmented chord, say C+ (C-E-G♯) and raise it up an octave, you still get a chord composed of two major thirds. The new chord is called E+ (E-G♯-B♯), and so on. Each augmented chord, therefore, is actually three chords in one.

Sixth Chords

A sixth or "6" chord is made up of a triad plus the note a major sixth up from the root. A C6 chord is C-E-G-A; a G6 chord is G-B-D-E; a D6 chord is D-F♯-A-B, and so on. If you drop the major sixth note an octave, the chord becomes a minor seventh chord. For example, taking the A in a C6 down an octave yields an Am7 chord (A-C-E-G).

Partial Barring with the Third or Fourth Fingers

To increase the number of strings that can be stopped for a given chord or fingering form, guitarists sometimes use the underside of the third or fourth finger end joints to perform partial barres. To make this possible, an end joint must be allowed to go flat, or even concave, relative to the middle joint of the finger. Sometimes these partial barres are performed in conjunction with a full or partial first-finger barre.

Third- and fourth-finger partial barres are indicated in fingering or chord diagrams by a horizontal "barre line" accompanied by a number (3 or 4) indicating the finger to be used.

Jazz Chords

Guitarists use the name *jazz chords* to describe a large body of movable standard forms for compound and altered chords. Most of these forms do not hit every note of a chord, but are actually partial chords that focus on "strategic notes." Figure 7–4 shows some frequently used jazz chords in first position. Each time a chord is raised a fret, the pitch of the entire chord goes up half a step. The notation above the tablature staff gives the name of the first position form plus a Roman numeral to show at which fret it is played. An indication above the standard notation staff shows the actual pitch of the chord. Observe that some jazz chords use third- and fourth-finger partial barres.

Figure 7–4

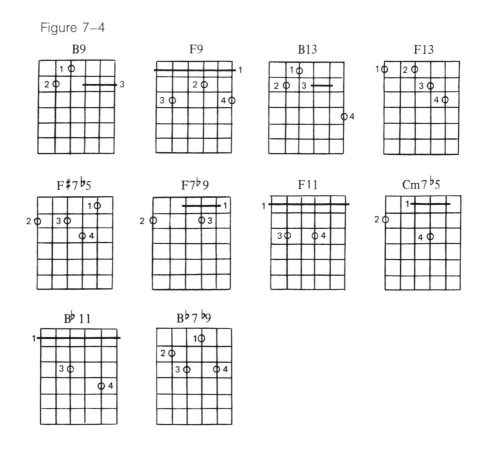

Andy Polon

Andy Polon is a versatile guitarist, teacher, and singer-songwriter from New York City. He learned country blues and ragtime guitar from Reverend Gary Davis and is very much at home in these idioms. He has also studied and become quite adept in rock, jazz, and classical guitar styles. During the 1970s, he was a well-known performer on the then-substantial New York area coffee house circuit. He now performs extensively throughout the northeastern United States and tours occasionally in Great Britain and western Europe.

Andy spends a considerable portion of his time working in ensemble settings. He has played with numerous bands, done a substantial amount of studio work and accompanied such well-known artists as Mary Travers (of Peter, Paul, and Mary) and Raun Mackinnon. His solo album, *Mad Metropolis* is on ADP records.

"Andy's Augmented Rag" is an original guitar piece by Andy Polon, so named because of the prominent augmented and augmented seventh chords in part A.[4] The tune is definitely a cross between Reverend Gary Davis style blues guitar and chord-melody style guitar. Note the frequent use of jazz chord forms (see figure 7–4) throughout the piece, the use of a third-finger barre in part A, measures 1, 2, and 3, and the use of a fourth-finger barre in measure 5 of the coda. If you're already familiar with jazz forms, the piece is not substantially harder than most conventional alternating bass pieces. If not, it will probably take you awhile to learn all the forms and play the tune fluidly. Fingering diagrams are in figure 7–5.

Figure 7–5

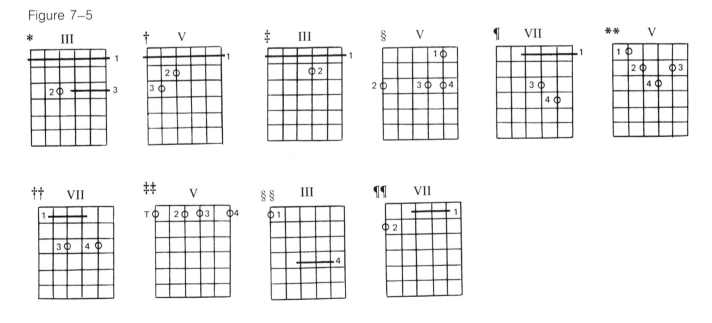

4"Andy's Augmented Rag," © 1985 by Andrew D. Polon.

Andy's Augmented Rag

Standard tuning
Key: C major

♩ = 108

by Andy Polon

(continued)

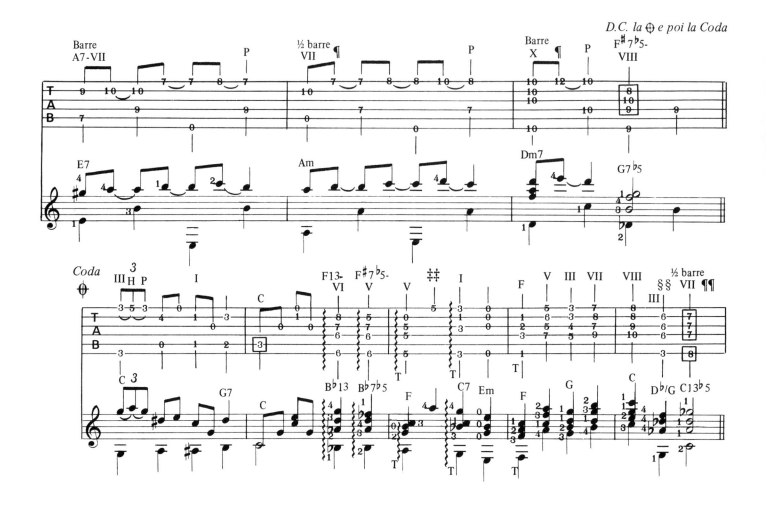

Rubato, a Tempo

Rubato is a musical direction indicating a nonmetronomic tempo. Instead of playing a tune with a rock-solid beat, the player toys with the rhythm. In some instances, the player slows down a series of notes (leaves a longer space between notes); in other instances, the player speeds up a series of notes (shortens the spaces between notes). This process is done more or less by feel and is fairly difficult to bring off effectively. Listen to some recordings of fingerpickers you admire and see if you can distinguish the rubato passages. Eventually, this should give you sufficient background to play rubato passages convincingly. The direction *a tempo* indicates that the piece is moving from rubato to a metronomic (rock-solid) beat.

Sixteenth-Note and Quarter-Note Triplets

The conventional triplet (also called an *eighth-note triplet*) is a group of three notes played in the space of a quarter note (one beat in $\frac{4}{4}$, $\frac{3}{4}$, or $\frac{2}{4}$ time). Other kinds of triplets exist and appear from time to time in guitar music. A *sixteenth-note triplet* (figure 7–6a) is a group of three notes played in the space of an eighth note (one half beat in $\frac{4}{4}$, $\frac{3}{4}$, or $\frac{2}{4}$ time). A *quarter-note triplet* (figure 7–6b) is a group of three notes played in the space of a half note (two beats in $\frac{4}{4}$, $\frac{3}{4}$, or $\frac{2}{4}$ time).

Figure 7–6a

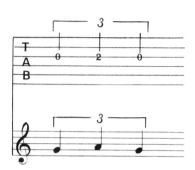

Figure 7–6b

The best way to count quarter-note triplets in $\frac{4}{4}$ time is to treat the measure as if it were in cut time ($\frac{2}{2}$). As you know, in cut time (Chapter 6) there are two beats per measure with half notes counting as one beat. In effect, each beat in $\frac{2}{2}$ divides the measure exactly in half, with each half representing two $\frac{4}{4}$ time beats. With the measure neatly divided in half, it's a relatively easy task to divide one or both of these halves into thirds.

Weak Harmonics

The most frequently used harmonics—found at the wire bordering the upper end of the fifth, seventh, and twelfth frets on any string—are known as *strong harmonics*. Other harmonics can be obtained, with some coaxing, over just about any fretwire. These additional harmonics are known as *weak harmonics* because their tone is substantially less powerful than the tone produced by strong harmonics. Notation for most weak harmonics is identical to that described in Chapter 4 for strong harmonics.

"8ᵛᵉ" HARMONICS

As you approach the nut, very high harmonic tones are obtainable *between fretwires*. These are notated by placing an octave (8^{ve}) sign over a conventional harmonic notation, as in the last measure of "The Way You Look in the Dark." Your job is then to hunt around the first couple of frets until you find a harmonic tone an octave higher than the notated harmonic. For example, if you have an "8^{ve}" notation above a harmonic on fret 5, string 1 (high A), you need to find a harmonic pitched one octave above the fret 5, string 1 harmonic. Since the fret 5, string 1 harmonic is two octaves above open high E, you need to find a pitch *three* octaves above open high E. With a little searching about, you can locate this harmonic slightly to the nutside of the second fretwire.

Closed Melodic Fingering Patterns

Melodic fingering patterns are fingering forms that yield runs of melody notes when combined with open strings (Chapter 3). Melodic fingering patterns can also be constructed that have *no* open strings. These *closed melodic patterns* usually call for substantial finger stretches, but the interesting tonality they impart to the guitar makes them well worth the trouble. Since the sounds produced by all the strings in a melodic fingering pattern should be allowed to overlap, all notes in that pattern must be kept firmly stopped throughout the duration of the run.

Colin Linden

Colin Linden of Toronto, Ontario, Canada, is one of the few players who use a fingerpicking style on both acoustic and electric guitars. He is equally at home in the country blues, rhythm and blues, and rock-'n'-roll idioms. He has performed extensively in Canada and the northern United States with his band and as a soloist, and he has an album with Ready Records called *Colin Linden Live*. He has played behind such notables as David Wilcox and Leon Redbone and has been employed as lead guitarist on several albums by a number of artists, such as Amos Garrett (*Amos Behavin* on Stony Plain), Mendelson Joe (*Jack Frost* and *Let's Party* on Boot), Morgan Davis (*I'm Ready to Play* on Bullhead), and Sam Chatman (*Sam Chatman & the Barbecue Boys* on Flying Fish).

Colin took up the guitar in 1970 at age 10, discovered blues music at 11, and started performing at 12. In his early teens he had the opportunity to meet and befriend the great blues artist Howlin' Wolf, from whom he first learned about the country blues and ragtime styles. He also learned about fingerpicking from Toronto guitarist John Thibodeau. He became a full-time musician at age 16.

In recent years, Colin has devoted himself primarily to songwriting and to recording this original material with his own music group.

"The Way You Look in the Dark" is an appealing tone portrait written for guitar by Colin Linden.[5] The tune is based on chord-melody ideas, and its overall sound is, as Colin describes it, "a cross between ragtime and R & B [rhythm and blues] music." Colin built the piece around a number of creative compound and altered chord voicings that work out to be either open or closed melodic fingering patterns. These patterns lead onto each other via suspension or voice leading, and the effect is extremely rich and evocative.

For example, the voicing for the E11 chord in measure 5 (marked with a double dagger) is a closed melodic fingering pattern. This moves via suspension to an AMaj7 voicing (section mark) that is an open melodic fingering pattern. The Amaj7 is followed by a D9 voicing that serves as another open pattern, and so on. Note the rubato sections in measures 1–4 and in measures 17–25 of the coda. Observe also the sixteenth-note triplets in measure 2 and in measures 11 and 22 of the coda, the quarter-note triplets in measure 24 of the coda, and the weak harmonics in measures 24 and 25 of the coda. Fingering diagrams are in figure 7–7.

Figure 7–7

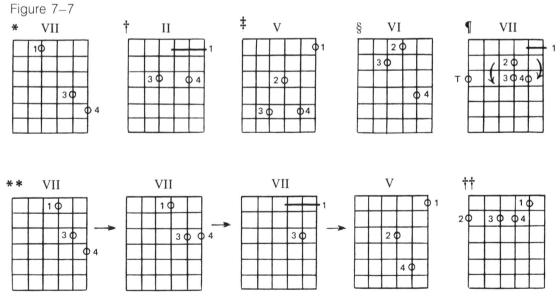

[5]"The Way You Look in the Dark," © 1985 by Colin Linden.

The Way You Look in the Dark

Standard tuning
Key: E major

♩ = 66

by Colin Linden

176

Coda

(continued)

178

TECHNIQUE

Double Hammer-ons and Pull-offs on Fretted Strings In measure 11 and in measures 14 and 16 of the coda, you are asked to stop a four-string form (marked with a reversed paragraph sign) and then hammer on at once to two fretted strings. To get the right sound, you'll have to practice keeping firm pressure on the stopped form with fingers T, 1, and 2, while fingers 3 and 4 perform a strong simultaneous H on strings 2 and 3.

In measure 11 of the coda, there is a double fretted pull-off on strings 1 and 3. To get the right sound, stop all four notes (two plucked notes and two P-notes) at the same time. Keep the P-notes (fret 5, string 1 and fret 6, string 3—A and C♯) firmly stopped as you pull off both plucked notes (fret 7, string 1 and fret 7, string 3—B and D) simultaneously.

Modulation and the Circle of Fifths

A key change within a piece of music is known as a *modulation*. When the modulation is long-lived, the key signature (Appendix A) is changed. If not, the key change is indicated by a trial of tell-tale accidentals.

All movement to circle-of-fifths double dominants, triple dominants, and the like is considered a form of modulation. For example, when a double dominant chord (say D or D7 in the key of C major) leads to a dominant chord (G or G7), that dominant chord in effect becomes the new tonic chord of the passage (see pp. 102 and 157). Until such time as the G-chord resumes its role as the dominant of C (leads back to a C-chord harmony), the key of the piece is officially considered to be G major.

CHROMATIC MODULATIONS

Chromatic modulations are noncircle-of-fifths key changes effected via voice leading. For example, taking an entire triad up or down a half step is an ideal voice-leading situation that appears frequently in guitar music. Each time a triad is moved in this manner, the new chord in effect becomes the tonic chord of a new key. In "Big Road Blues," for example (see Chapter 5), when the harmony changes from D to D♭, the D♭ major chord actually becomes the tonic of the passage. The tune is then considered to be in the key of D♭ major until such time as the harmony moves from a D♭ chord back to a D chord.

Alternatively, one or two voices in a chord can be raised or lowered a half step to form the nucleus of a new chord, even when the new chord is far away from the original chord on the circle of fifths.

This new chord is then considered the tonic chord of the passage until the next modulation occurs.

In part D, measures 12–13 of "Paragon Rag," for example, the harmony moves from C chord (C-E-G) to an A♭ chord (A♭-C-E♭) by way of voice leading (G to A♭, E to E♭) and a suspension (C to C). A♭ is then considered the tonic of the passage until the middle of measure 14, when the key returns via chromatic modulation to C major. As you might expect, chromatic modulations are usually accompanied by a large number of accidentals. The names of the chords involved can then be determined by examining their spelling.

No collection of fingerstyle guitar tunes would be complete without at least one classic piano rag transcription. For this volume, I've arranged Scott Joplin's "Paragon Rag." This tune, which was first published in 1909 by Seminary Music Co. of New York, appears in a modern volume called *Scott Joplin: Collected Piano Works*. A fine version of the tune is played by Joshua Rifkin on his album, *Piano Rags by Scott Joplin, Volume II*. In his linear notes, Rifkin observes that "'Paragon Rag' unites the exuberance of [Joplin's] earlier music with a mature subtlety of detail."

This arrangement is based on the original piano music and is in the original piano keys (G major and C major). Fingering diagrams are in figure 7–8.

Figure 7–8

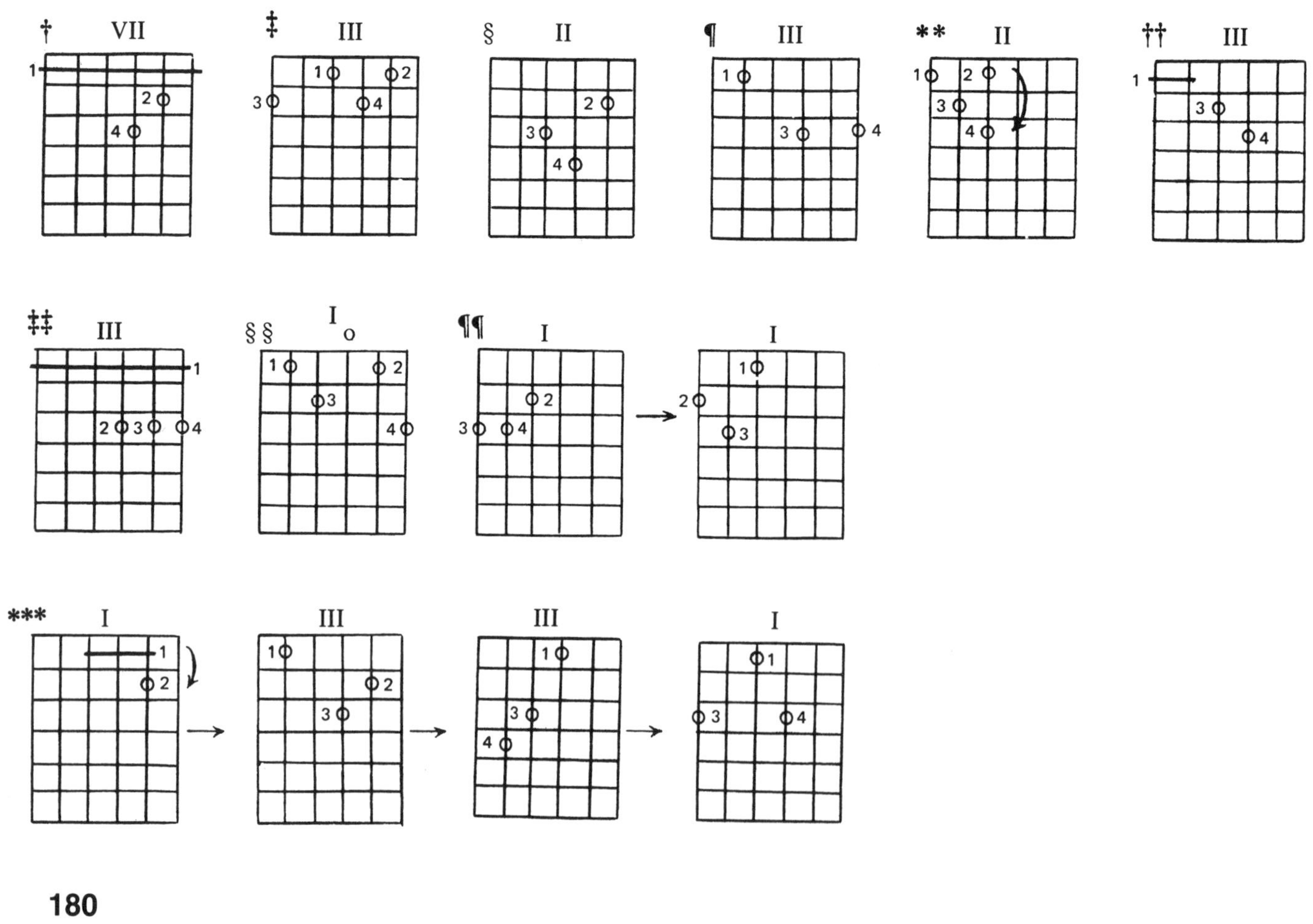

180

Paragon Rag

Standard tuning
Keys: Parts A ab Б: G major
Parts C and D: C major

𝅗𝅥 = 63

by Scott Joplin
arranged by Ken Perlman

(continued)

Reprise Part A

Reprise Part A

End, Reprise

Part C

(continued)

Erik Frandsen

Erik Frandsen has been an integral part of the Greenwich Village Folk Music scene since the late 1960s. His mastery of the guitar has earned him the nickname "The Old Professor" and the respect of his peers. He has backed up many performers in New York and on tour (often using such aliases as Fresno Slim) and has performed extensively as a solo artist throughout the eastern half of the United States. One of his banjo compositions appears in my *Melodic Clawhammer Banjo* book.

Erik took up the guitar in the early 1960s. He studied country blues style by listening to recordings of such players as Robert Johnson, Lightnin' Hopkins, and Spike Jones, and he is generally considered to be a master of the idiom. In recent years he has turned a good deal of his energy to guitar composition. Erik has these words to say for himself:

"Erik Frandsen was a disc jockey at the age of 15, has played as well as M.C.'d countless concerts and festivals, done many recording sessions, acted on Broadway, and was once a wheelman for the notorious Danny "Extreme Unction" Shea. He lives in New York City. He needs work. He is in the phone book."

"Mary-Joan or the Siege of Leningrad" is an Erik Frandsen composition.[6] Erik notes that it was "written for my favorite actress and frequent muse, Mary-Joan Negro, as a consolation prize for being in a bad Russian play."

The piece is quite long and structured loosely with four parts of varying length. Each section has a different theme, but short motifs reappear frequently throughout the work. The piece is held together by a well-conceived bass line, which takes the player via voice leading through a large number of interesting and unusual harmonies. This style of composition is very reminiscent of Baroque music, and the piece can be thought of as a hybrid of the country blues and baroque musical styles. Erik describes it as "a 17th Century English pastoral Disco Bossa-Nova Gavotte. Mostly English, but it does contain elements of French, Russian, Italian, Roquefort, and Thousand Islands."

Erik, who is noted for his wit, has offered a musical direction to go with each part. Part A has the direction "Al Dente" (with bite), part B has the direction "Con Brillo" (with steel wool), part C has the direction "Con Molto Calamari" (with lots of squid), and part D has the direction "Drāno." Fingering diagrams for the tune appear in figure 7–9.

6"Mary-Joan or the Siege of Leningrad," © 1985 by Erik Frandsen.

Figure 7-9

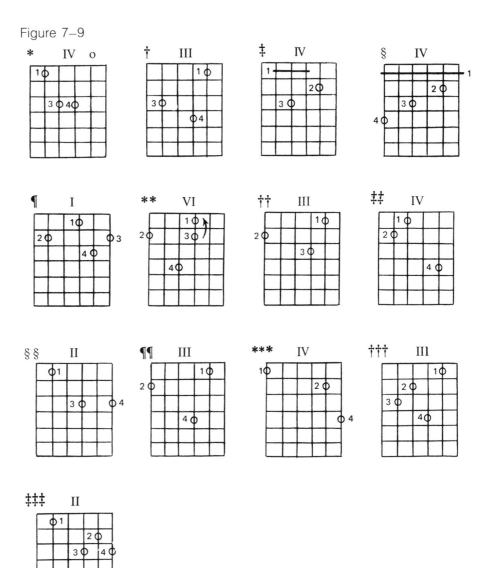

Mary-Joan or the Siege of Leningrad

Standard tuning
Key: A major

♩ = 69

by Erik Frandsen

(continued)

(continued)

D.C. al ⊕ e poi la Coda   *Coda*

TECHNIQUE

Different Length Measures and Cut Time   In cut time, a half note counts as one beat and there are two beats per measure. The signature $\frac{1}{2}$ then, indicates a measure with one cut-time beat, while $\frac{3}{2}$ signifies a measure with three cut-time beats.

Besides one $\frac{3}{2}$ and a number of $\frac{1}{2}$ measures, this piece also includes one $\frac{1}{4}$ and a couple of $\frac{3}{4}$ measures. The $\frac{1}{4}$ measure has a duration of half a cut-time beat (the length of one quarter note) while the $\frac{3}{4}$ measures last one and a half cut-time beats (the length of a dotted half note). Remember that the first beat of every measure is *always* accented, no matter how many beats are within it.

Playing Open Treble Notes under a Full Barre   In part A, measure 6 and in a number of other locations, you are asked to play an open treble string (say string 2) while holding on to a barred bass note (in this case, fret 2, string 5, or low B). To accomplish this, keep your first finger in barring position, but raise up your arm and thrust your wrist out considerably. This will permit you to lift the attached joint of your barring finger off the treble strings, while still maintaining pressure on the bass strings.

Nick Katzman

Nick Katzman is an outstanding guitarist and gifted composer from New York City. He has accompanied such blues singers as Terry Garthwaite, Rachel Faro, and Rory Block (Chapter 5) and has performed extensively as a solo artist both in the New York City area and in the San Francisco Bay area of California. His two albums recorded for Kicking Mule—*Mississippi River Bottom Blues* and *Sparkling Ragtime and Hardbitten Blues*—feature a number of exquisite original guitar instrumentals.

Nick was born in Paris, but his family moved to New York soon afterwards. He studied blues guitar in the mid-1960s with Reverend Gary Davis and Stefan Grossman. One powerful influence he mentions was the experience of being a young guitarist at the Newport (Rhode Island) Folk Festivals of 1965 and 66, where he was able to hear and learn from such legendary blues masters as Mississippi John Hurt, Son House, and Skip James.

Starting in the early 70s, Nick embarked on a formal study of the guitar. He took lessons in theory, classical guitar, and jazz guitar, and he even learned to play the baroque lute. By combining these formal influences with his country blues background, he has developed a powerful, crystal-clear yet lyrical style of playing and composing.

Nick also plays pick-style Chicago blues guitar. As lead guitarist in the backup band for New York bluesman Guitar Crusher, he has spent the last couple of years on tour in West Germany.

"Philosophy Rag" is a Nick Katzman original, appearing on his *Sparkling Ragtime and Hardbitten Blues* album (Kicking Mule).[7] Nick writes, "It's more of a chordal rag than a melodic one. It involves unusual harmonies and deceptive cadences, and though based on classic piano rag composition, it makes use of devices and musical approaches unique to the guitar."

The piece shows a wealth of musical influences. There are, of course, melodic ideas and stylistic devices borrowed from classic ragtime. In addition, Nick borrows ideas and conventions from the country blues, baroque music, and even Gershwin. He has structured the piece roughly like a classic rag, but there are some notable differences. Classic rags, as you know, have four repeated 16-measure parts. In "Philosophy Rag," part A, which is *not* reprised between parts B and C, is 24 measures long. Part C is 23 measures long and not repeated, while part D is only nine measures long. In most classic rags, part C moves to a new key. In this piece, part B begins on the relative minor key (F♯ minor) and ends on a new key (D major). Parts C and D return to the original A major key. Observe the continual circle-of-fifths and chromatic modulations throughout the piece. Observe also the constant use of unique fingering forms and creative chord voicings.

The third ending of part A is to be used *only* as the coda of the piece. Fingering diagrams are in figure 7–10.

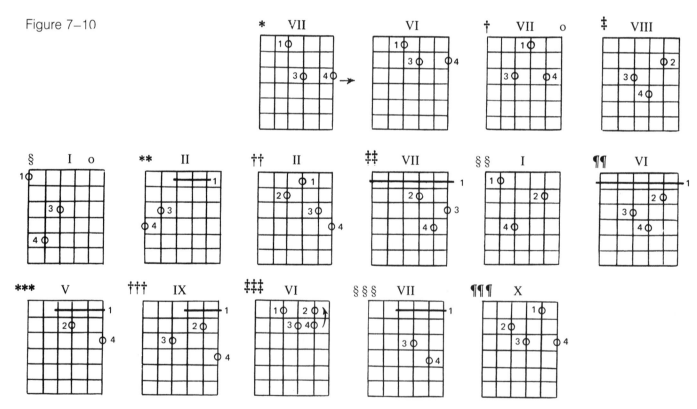

Figure 7–10

[7]"Philosophy Rag," by Nick Katzman, © 1979 by Kicking Mule Publishing Co., Inc. Used by permission.

Philosophy Rag

Standard tuning

Keys: Parts A, C, D: A major
       Part B: F♯ minor, D major

♩ = 63

by Nick Katzman

(continued)

196

(continued)

TECHNIQUE

Playing Open Bass Notes under a Full Barre   In part B, measures 1, 2, 4, and 9, there are open bass notes in the middle of barred fingering forms. This means that you must maintain pressure on the treble strings with the underside of part of the first finger, while rocking the fingertip up off the fretboard over the bass strings.

8
Appendices

Appendix A:
Notes, Scales, and Keys

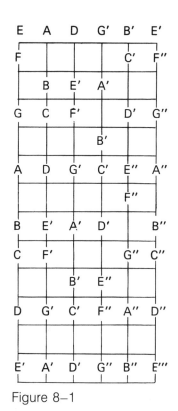

Figure 8–1

Most European and American music is based on a scale of seven tones, each named for a letter of the alphabet:

A B C D E F G

These tones repeat over and over again at higher and lower levels. So after any G, there is another A (followed by a B, a C, and so on). Before any A, there is another G (preceded by an F, an E, and so on). The distance from any tone to the next higher or lower same-letter tone is called an *octave*. The guitar has a *range* of nearly four octaves; the piano has a range of nearly seven octaves, and so on.

These seven tones (A–G) are called *natural notes*. When played in order for the distance of one octave *from any starting point* (A-B-C-D-E-F-G-A, C-D-E-F-G-A-B-C, and so on), these notes form a *diatonic scale*.

Figure 8–1 shows a fingerboard diagram for the first 12 frets of a guitar in standard tuning. Natural notes are listed in the locations where they occur. Notes in the low octave (low E, low F, and so on) are shown without primes, notes in the middle octave (middle E, middle F, and so on) are shown with one prime, notes in the high octave (high E, high F) are shown with two primes, and notes in the very-high octave are shown with three primes. Observe that a single pitch can occur at a number of different locations on the fingerboard.

By convention, notes on the guitar are written one octave *above* their actual pitch. Low E's actual pitch is two E's below middle C on the piano, but it is written as one E below middle C. High E's actual pitch is E above middle C on the piano, but it is written as two E's above middle C. The *written* pitch of the guitar's open strings is shown in figure 8–2.

Figure 8–2

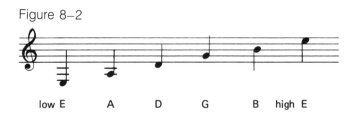

low E   A   D   G   B high E

202

MAJOR, MINOR, AND MODAL SCALES

The first widely used diatonic scales were what we now refer to as *modal* scales. These include the Dorian scale (D-E-F-G-A-B-C-D), the Phrygian scale (E-F-G-A-B-C-D-E), the Lydian scale (F-G-A-B-C-D-E-F), `and the Mixolydian scale (G-A-B-C-D-E-F-G). These scales still appear frequently in American and European folk music.

The major scale (do - re - mi - fa - so - la - ti - do) and the natural minor scale came into general use a few hundred years ago. The all-natural-note major scale is C-D-E-F-G-A-B-C, while the all-natural-note minor scale (also called the Aeolian mode) is A-B-C-D-E-F-G-A.

SHARPS AND FLATS
(THE CHROMATIC SCALE)

Look again at figure 8–1 and observe that some natural notes are one fret (a *half step*) apart, while most others are two frets (a *whole step*) apart. The notes found on the frets between the natural notes are known as sharps (♯) and flats (♭). For example, the note between C and D is known as C♯ or D♭; the note between F and G is called F♯ or G♭, and so on. A series of notes that includes all the natural notes and sharps and flats for the distance of one octave is called a chromatic scale. Observe in figure 8–1 and in the following C chromatic scale (figure 8-3), that the notes E–F and B–C are only a half step (one fret) apart and have no *intervening* sharps and flats.

Figure 8–3

KEYS

If you take the all-natural-note major scale (C-D-E-F-G-A-B-C) and compare it to the C chromatic scale you'll observe that the sequence of whole steps and half steps is as follows: whole, whole, half, whole, whole, whole, half. Only a natural diatonic scale beginning on C has this particular order of whole and half steps. By using sharps or flats, however, you can start from any natural note (or even from a sharp or flat) and create the same order of whole and half steps.

Each series of notes with this order of whole and half steps is then a major scale in its own right, and the starting note, known as the *key* or *tonic* note, determines the *key* of the scale. For example, a major scale beginning on G (called a major scale in the key of G, or simply G *major*) runs G-A-B-C-D-E-F♯-G; a D-major scale runs D-E-F♯-G-

A-B-C#-D; an A-major scale runs A-B-C#-D-E-F#-G#-A, an F-major scale runs F-G-A-B♭-C-D-E-F, a B♭ major scale runs B♭-C-D-E♭-F-G-A-B♭, and so on.

Similar principles can be applied to constructing minor and modal scales in the various keys. The all-natural-note D Dorian scale (D-E-F-G-A-B-C-D) for example, runs whole (step), half, whole, whole, whole, half, whole. An A Dorian scale then, is A-B-C-D-E-F#-G-A, an E Dorian scale is E-F#-G-A-B-C#-D-E, and so on. The all-natural-note G Mixolydian scale (G-A-B-C-D-E-F-G) runs whole, whole, half, whole, whole, half, whole. A D Mixolydian scale, then, is D-E-F#-G-A-B-C-D; an A Mixolydian scale is A-B-C#-D-E-F#-G-A, and so on. The all-natural-note A Aeolian (natural minor) scale (A-B-C-D-E-F-G-A) runs whole, half, whole, whole, half, whole, whole. An E minor (Aeolian) scale, then, is E-F#-G-A-B-C-D-E; a B minor scale is B-C#-D-E-F#-G-A-B, and so on.

KEY SIGNATURES AND RELATIVE KEYS

Key signatures are placed at the start of each *line* of music to indicate the key of that line. A signature of no sharps or flats, for example, indicates an all-natural-note scale (C-major, D Dorian, and so on). By examining the overall sound of the piece and, in particular, the concluding measure or two, it is usually easy to determine which natural-note scale is indicated. One hint: The very last note of a tune is usually the tonic note of that tune. Another hint: Since more than 90 percent of the music you're likely to encounter is in a major key, *assume the piece is major unless there are strong indications to the contrary.* All scales with the same key signature are called *relative keys.*

Figure 8–4   Relative Keys

KEY SIGNATURES	MAJOR	MINOR	DORIAN	MIXOLYDIAN
no # or ♭	C	A	D	G
F#	G	E	A	D
F#, C#	D	B	E	A
F#, C#, G#	A	F#	B	E
F#, C#, G#, D#	E	C#	F#	B
F#, C#, G#, D#, A#	B	G#	C#	F#
F#, C#, G#, D#, A#, E#	F#	D#	G#	C#
B♭	F	D	G	C
B♭, E♭	B♭	G	C	F
B♭, E♭, A♭	E♭	C	F	B♭
B♭, E♭, A♭, D♭	A♭	F	B♭	E♭
B♭, E♭, A♭, D♭, G♭	D♭	B♭	E♭	A♭
B♭, E♭, A♭, D♭, G♭, C♭	G♭	E♭	A♭	C♭

Similarly, a signature of one sharp (always F♯) indicates all the diatonic scales made of six natural notes and F♯, such as G-major, A Dorian, E minor, and so on, all of which are considered relative keys. Figure 8–4 shows some key signatures and some of the relative keys they indicate.

Appendix B:
A Daily Exercise Routine

A 10- to 20-minute exercise routine to warm up your fingers is an excellent prelude to daily practice. I'll discuss right- and left-hand exercises separately. I'm not suggesting you do all of these every day. Experiment with all of them until you find a routine that's right for you.

RIGHT-HAND EXERCISES

Daily Fingerpicking Exercises (see Chapter 4). *Time:* about five minutes.

Arpeggio Exercises There's a standard work called *120 Exercises for the Right Hand* by Mauro Giulianni. Learn about 10 exercises per week (each is only two measures long). Once you are familiar with all the exercises, run through about 20 or 30 per day as a warmup. *Time:* about five minutes.

LEFT-HAND EXERCISES

Segovia Scales A book called *Diatonic Major and Minor Scales* by Andres Segovia is very helpful in learning the fingerboard, facilitating position shifts, achieving left-hand agility, and mastering a four-fret stretch at each position. Learn one or two scales per week. Once thoroughly learned, all 24 major and minor scales can be played through in less than 10 minutes.

Jazz Guitar Scales A Modern Method for Guitar (Volumes 1–3) by William Leavitt presents a collection of scales with a basic four-fret stretch that often calls for a five-fret stretch. After a few five-fret stretches, a four-fret stretch seems like a piece of cake! The book is intended for flatpick style, but you can play through the scales by alternating your plucking-hand fingers in the manner suggested by the Segovia book. Read through one or two scale series a day. *Time:* less than five minutes.

H and P Exercises See *Fingerstyle Guitar*, Chapters 8 and 9 and this book, Chapter 6. I suggest that you run through the "Hammer-on and Pull-off Warmup" (Chapter 6) every day. For even more agility, play the other exercises as well. *Time:* five to ten minutes.

Appendix C: Nail Care

If you're going to pick with your nails, you'd better get used to the idea of devoting considerable energy to keeping them in playing shape. The nail grows out from the finger with sharp corners. These must be filed so that the edge of the nail takes on a semicircular shape. The best tool to use for this purpose is an "emeryll" or "diamond" file (a metal file coated with fine particles). After filing, the edge of a nail should extend about one-eighth of an inch past the fingertip and about a quarter of an inch past the thumbtip.

To prevent tearing of the nail while playing or during routine use, file any tiny nicks or dents smooth with #500 or #600 Carbide (wet-and-dry) paper, which is available in hardware stores. If you have soft or brittle nails, you can assist nature by applying a *nail conditioner* on both inside and outside of the nail anywhere from once a week to once a day. Nail conditioners, which are *not* shiny, contain gelatinlike substances that sink in and add mass to the nail. For safety's sake, avoid brands that contain formaldehyde.

Appendix D: Metronomes

Metronomes are clocklike devices designed to click at a constant rate. This rate can be altered by spinning a dial or moving a metal weight along a shaft to various marked settings. A metronome setting of 72, for example, causes the machine to click 72 times per minute. Musicians play a tune or exercise at the rate of one beat per click. By increasing the setting, the metronome beats faster, and the musician is constrained to play at a quicker pace.

Notation using metronome settings is a useful way of indicating the ideal tempo for various tunes. The kind of note counted as one beat is determined (quarter notes in $\frac{4}{4}$ time, half notes in cut time, and so on), then equated with a metronome setting as follows:

$\quad \quad$ ♩ = 96

$\quad \quad$ 𝅗𝅥 = 60

$\quad \quad$ ♩. = 72

The top entry means that a $\frac{4}{4}$, $\frac{3}{4}$, or $\frac{2}{4}$ tune should be played at a speed at which each beat coincides with a click on a metronome set at 96; the second entry means that a cut-time tune should be played at a speed at which each beat coincides with a click on a metronome set at 60. The third entry applies to meters like $\frac{6}{8}$, $\frac{9}{8}$, or $\frac{12}{8}$, where one click covers the space of an entire eighth-note group (three eighth notes equal one dotted quarter note). It indicates that a piece is to be played at a speed at which the beginning of each group coincides with a click on a metronome set at 72.

Discography

Pink Anderson: Medicine Show Man. Prestige/Bluesville 1051.

Geoff Bartley: Blues Beneath the Surface. Magic Crow 1001.

BENSUSAN, PIERRE.
  Près de Paris. Rounder 3023.
  Pierre Bensusan #2. Rounder 3037.
  Musiques. Rounder 3038.
  Solilai. Rounder 3068.

Berkeley Farms. Folkways FA 2436.

Berkeley Out West. Arhoolie 4001.

Blind Blake: Bootleg Rum Dum Blues. Biograph BLP-12003.

Allan Block: Alive and Well and Fiddlin'. Living Folk 104.

BLOCK, RORY.
  Intoxication. Chrysalis CHR-1157.
  You're the One. Chrysalis CHR-1233.
  High Heeled Blues. Rounder 3061.
  Blue Horizon. Rounder 3073.
  Rhinestones and Steel Strings. Rounder
  Rory Block and Stefan Grossman: How to Play Blues Guitar. Kicking Mule

Boys of the Lough: Lochaber No More. Philo 1031.

Big Bill Broonzy: 1930's Blues. Biograph BLP-C15.

Gill Burns: Aloan at Last. No Such GEB-8751.

Howie Bursen: Cider in the Kitchen. Folk Legacy FSI-74.

Sam Chatman and the Barbecue Boys. Flying Fish.

The Chieftains #2. Claddaugh TA4.

Charlie Christian. Everest FS-219.

Lynn Clayton. Airship AP85.

Michael Coleman: The Legacy of Michael Coleman. Shanachie 33002.

Contemporary Ragtime Guitar. Kicking Mule.

Reverend Gary Davis. Yazoo L-1023.

Morgan Davis: I'm Ready to Play. Bullhead.

The Delmore Brothers: Brown's Ferry Blues. (County 402)

John Fahey: Old Fashioned Love. Takoma C-1043.

Archie Fischer: Man With a Rhyme. Folk Legacy FSS61.

Amos Garrett: Amos Behavin. Stony Plain.

Wendy Grossman: Roseville Fair. Lincoln House LHR 68001. (Available from Silo Records).

Lightnin' Hopkins. Arhoolie F1022.

Son House: The Real Delta Blues. Blue Goose 2016.

Mississippi John Hurt: 1928 Sessions. Yazoo 1065.

Blind Lemon Jefferson: 1926–9 Vols. 1 and 2. Biograph BLP-12015.

JENKS, GLENN.

    Antidote. Bonnie Banks 102.

    Background Music. Fretless 157.

    The Ragtime Project. Bonnie Banks 103.

Lonnie Johnson: Mr. Johnson's Blues. Mamlish 53807.

Robert Johnson: King of the Delta Blues Singers. Columbia CL 1654

KAIRO, PETE.

    Playing it Safe. Physical World PR32-006.

    Hanging Out. Physical World PR32-014.

KATZMAN, NICK.

    Mississippi River Bottom Blues. Kicking Mule KM111.

    Sparkling Ragtime and Hardbitten Blues. Kicking Mule.

Jo-Anne Kelly. Blue Goose 2009.

B. B. King: Live at the Regal. ABC Paramount ABCS-509.

Leadbelly: Take This Hammer. Folkways 31019.

Colin Linden: Colin Linden Live. Ready L-1011.

Andy McGann and Paddy Reynolds. Shanachie 29004.

Brownie McGhee and Sonny Terry: Browny and Sonny. Everest FS-242.

Willie McTell: The Early Years. Yazoo L-1005.

MENDELSON, JOE.

    Jack Frost. Boot.

    Let's Party. Boot.

Melange. Amsterdam Folk Collective

Jelly Roll Morton: Piano Classics, 1923–4. Folkways RF-47.

Old Time Fiddle Classics. County 507.

Charlie Patton: Founder of the Delta Blues. Yazoo L-1020.

Ken Perlman: Clawhammer Banjo & Fingerstyle Guitar Solos. Folkways FTS 31098.

Andy Polon: Mad Metropolis. ADP 101.

Malvina Reynolds: Artichokes, Griddle Cakes, and Other Good Things. Pacific Cascades LPL-7081.

Joshua Rifkin: Piano Rags by Scott Joplin, Vol. II. Nonesuch H-71264.

SEEGER, PETE.

    Singalong. Folkways FXM-36055.

    Circles and Seasons. Warner Bros. BSK-3329.

    The Bitter and the Sweet. Columbia CL-1916.

    Circles and Seasons. Warner Bros. BSK-3329.

    The Bitter and the Sweet. Columbia CL-1916.

    Arlo Guthrie and Pete Seeger: Precious Friend. Warner Bros. 2BSK-3644.

SMITH, JANET.

The Unicorn. Takoma A1027.

I'm a Delightful Child. Pacific Cascades LPL-7027.

Some People Who Play Guitar (Like a Lot of People Don't). Kicking Mule KM104.

Bill Steele: Chocolate Cookies. Swallowtail ST-8.

Taj Mahal: The Natch'l Blues. Columbia CS-9698.

TRAUM, HAPPY.

Relax Your Mind. Kicking Mule 110.

American Stranger. Kicking Mule 301.

Bright Mornin' Stars. Greenhays GR703.

Friends & Neighbors. Vest Pocket VP001.

Happy & Artie Traum: Hard Times in the Country. Rounder 3007.

VAN RONK, DAVE.

Dave Van Ronk, Folksinger. Prestige/Folklore 14012.

Dave Van Ronk Sings the Blues. Verve Folkways FVS-9006.

Just Dave Van Ronk. Mercury SR-60908.

Dave Van Ronk and the Jug Stompers. Mercury SR-60864.

Gambler's Blues. Verve Folkways FVS-9017.

Inside Dave Van Ronk. Prestige/Folklore 14025.

Sunday Street. Philo 1036.

Somebody Else, Not Me. Philo 1065.

The Weavers: Together Again. Loom 1681.

The Woman's Guitar Workshop. Kicking Mule 139.

Bibliography

BENSUSAN, PIERRE. *Le Livre de Guitare de Pierre Bensusan.* Paris: Published by Author, 1984. (U.S. distributor—Mike Savicki, 44 Howe St., Framingham, MA).

BLOCK, RORY AND GROSSMAN, STEFAN. *How to Play Blues Guitar.* Berkeley, CA: Kicking Mule Publishing, 1966.

CHRISTESON, R. P. *The Old Time Fiddler's Repertory.* Columbia, MO: University of Missouri Press, 1973.

GIULIANNI, MAURO. *120 Exercises for the Right Hand.* Italy: c. 1810. Available in several editions.

JOPLIN, SCOTT. *Collected Piano Works.* New York: New York Public Library, 1971.

LEAVITT, WILLIAM. A *Modern Method for the Guitar, Vols. I–III.* Boston: Berklee Press, 1966, 1968, 1971.

MANN, WOODY. *Early Blues Guitarists.* New York: Music Sales, 1973. "Fingerstyle Jazz Improvization" (tape series) New York: Guitar Workshop Co.

NOTE: The bibliography includes listing of instructional tapes.

O'Neill's Music of Ireland. Chicago, 1903. Reprinted New York: Dan Collins, 1973.

PERLMAN, KEN.

Clawhammer-Style Banjo. Englewood Cliffs, N.J.: Prentice-Hall, 1983.

Fingerpicking Fiddle Tunes: Traditional Dance Music Arranged for Fingerstyle Guitar. New York: Chappell Music, 1978.

Fingerstyle Guitar. Englewood Cliffs, N.J.: Prentice-Hall, 1980.

Melodic Clawhammer Banjo. New York: Oak Publications, 1979.

New England and Irish Fiddle Tunes for Clawhammer Banjo. New York: Chappell, 1980.

"Clawhammer Banjo" (tape series). Woodstock, NY: Homespun Tapes.

"Clawhammer Style Banjo" (videotape series). Dunlap, IL: Video Music Productions.

SEEGER, PETE. *How to Play the 5-String Banjo.* New York: Music Sales, 1961.

SEGOVIA, ANDRES. *Diatonic Major and Minor Scales.* Washington, D.C.: Columbia Music, 1953.

SHARPE, CECIL J. *The English Folk Song: Some Conclusions.* London: Simpkin, 1907.

SMITH, JANET. *Fingerstyle Guitar Solos.* Fullerton, CA: Centerstream Publishing, 1983.

TRAUM, HAPPY.

Fingerpicking Styles for Guitar. New York: Oak, 1966.

The Guitar of Brownie McGhee. New York: Oak, 1971.

Traditional and Contemporary Fingerpicking. New York: Oak, 1969.

"Fingerpicking Guitar" (tape series). Woodstock, NY. Homespun Tapes.

"Country Blues Guitar" (tapes series). Woodstock, NY. Homespun Tapes.

"Flatpick Country Guitar" (tape series). Woodstock, NY. Homespun Tapes.

Index

GUITAR INSTRUCTION & TECHNIQUE

THE GUITAR CHORD SHAPES OF CHARLIE CHRISTIAN
Book/CD Pack
by Joe Weidlich
The concepts and fingerings in this book have been developed by analyzing the licks used by Charlie Christian. Chord shapes are moveable; thus one can play the riffs in virtually any key without difficulty by simply moving the shape, and fingerings used to play them, up or down the fingerboard. The author shows how the chord shapes – F, D and A – are formed, then can easily be modified to major, minor, dominant seventh and diminished seventh chord voicings.†Analyzing licks frequently used by Charlie Christian, Joe has identified a series of what he calls tetrafragments, i.e., the core element of a lick. The identifiable "sound" of a particular lick is preserved regardless of how many notes are added on either side of it, e.g., pickup notes or tag endings.† Many examples are shown and played on the CD of how this basic concept was used by Charlie Christian to keep his solo lines moving forward. Weidlich also makes observations on the physical manner Charlie Christian used in playing jazz guitar and how that approach contributed to his smooth, mostly down stroke, pick technique.
00000388 Guitar $19.95

GUITAR CHORDS PLUS
by Ron Middlebrook
A comprehensive study of normal and extended chords, tuning, keys, transposing, capo use, and more. Includes over 500 helpful photos and diagrams, a key to guitar symbols, and a glossary of guitar terms.
00000011 ....$11.95

GUITAR TRANSCRIBING – A COMPLETE GUIDE
by Dave Celentano
Learn that solo now! Don't wait for the music to come out – use this complete guide to writing down what you hear. Includes tips, advice, examples and exercises from easy to difficult. Your ear is the top priority and you'll train it to listen more effectively to recognize intervals, chords, note values, counting rhythms and much more for an accurate transcription.
00000378 Book/CD Pack $19.95

GUITAR TUNING FOR THE COMPLETE MUSICAL IDIOT (FOR SMART PEOPLE TOO)
by Ron Middlebrook
A complete book on how to tune up. Contents include: Everything You Need To Know About Tuning; Intonation; Strings; 12-String Tuning; Picks; and much more.
00000002 ....$5.95

INTRODUCTION TO ROOTS GUITAR
by Doug Cox
This book/CD pack by Canada's premier guitar and Dobro® player introduces beginning to intermediate players to many of the basics of folk/roots guitar. Topics covered include: basic theory, tuning, reading tablature, right- and left-hand patterns, blues rhythms, Travis picking, frailing patterns, flatpicking, open tunings, slide and many more. CD includes 40 demonstration tracks.
00000262 Book/CD Pack $17.95
00000265 VHS Video $19.95

KILLER PENTATONICS FOR GUITAR
by Dave Celentano
Covers innovative and diverse ways of playing pentatonic scales in blues, rock and heavy metal. The licks and ideas in this book will give you a fresh approach to playing the pentatonic scale, hopefully inspiring you to reach for higher levels in your playing. The 37-minute companion CD features recorded examples.
00000285 Book/CD Pack $17.95

LEFT HAND GUITAR CHORD CHART
by Ron Middlebrook
Printed on durable card stock, this "first-of-a-kind" guitar chord chart displays all forms of major and minor chords in two forms, beginner and advanced.
00000005 ....$2.95

MELODIC LINES FOR THE INTERMEDIATE GUITARIST
by Greg Cooper
This book/CD pack is essential for anyone interested in expanding melodic concepts on the guitar. Author Greg Cooper covers: picking exercises; major, minor, dominant and altered lines; blues and jazz turn-arounds; and more.
00000312 Book/CD Pack $19.95

MELODY CHORDS FOR GUITAR
by Allan Holdsworth
Influential fusion player Allan Holdsworth provides guitarists with a simplified method of learning chords, in diagram form, for playing accompaniments and for playing popular melodies in "chord-solo" style. Covers: major, minor, altered, dominant and diminished scale notes in chord form, with lots of helpful reference tables and diagrams.
00000222 ....$19.95

MODAL JAMS AND THEORY
by Dave Celentano
This book shows you how to play the modes, the theory behind mode construction, how to play any mode in any key, how to play the proper mode over a given chord progression, and how to write chord progressions for each of the seven modes. The CD includes two rhythm tracks and a short solo for each mode so guitarists can practice with a "real" band.
00000163 Book/CD Pack $17.95

MONSTER SCALES AND MODES
by Dave Celentano
This book is a complete compilation of scales, modes, exotic scales, and theory. It covers the most common and exotic scales, theory on how they're constructed, and practical applications. No prior music theory knowledge is necessary, since every section is broken down and explained very clearly.
00000140 ....$7.95

OLD TIME COUNTRY GUITAR BACKUP BASICS
by Joseph Weidlich
This instructional book uses commercial recordings from 70 different "sides" from the 1920s and early 1930s as its basis to learn the principal guitar backup techniques commonly used in old-time country music. Topics covered include: boom-chick patterns • bass runs • uses of the pentatonic scale • rhythmic variations • minor chromatic nuances • the use of chromatic passing tones • licks based on chords or chord progressions • and more.
00000389 ....$15.95

OPEN GUITAR TUNINGS
by Ron Middlebrook
This booklet illustrates over 75 different tunings in easy-to-read diagrams. Includes tunings used by artists such as Chet Atkins, Michael Hedges, Jimmy Page, Joe Satriani and more for rock, blues, bluegrass, folk and country styles including open D (for slide guitar), Em, open C, modal tunings and many more.
00000130 ....$4.95

OPEN TUNINGS FOR GUITAR
by Dorian Michael
This book provides 14 folk songs in 9 tunings to help guitarists become comfortable with changing tunings. Songs are ordered so that changing from one tuning to another is logical and non-intrusive. Includes: Fisher Blues (DADGBE) • Fine Toast to Hewlett (DGDGBE) • George Barbazan (DGDGBD) • Amelia (DGDGCD) • Will the Circle Be Unbroken (DADF#AD) • more.
00000224 Book/CD Pack $19.95

ARRANGING FOR OPEN GUITAR TUNINGS
By Dorian Michael
This book/CD pack teaches intermediate-level guitarists how to choose an appropriate tuning for a song, develop an arrangement, and solve any problems that may arise while turning a melody into a guitar piece to play and enjoy.
00000313 Book/CD Pack $19.95

ROCK RHYTHM GUITAR
by Dave Celentano
This helpful book/CD pack cuts out all the confusing technical talk and just gives guitarists the essential tools to get them playing. With Celentano's tips, anyone can build a solid foundation of basic skills to play almost any rhythm guitar style. The exercises and examples are on the CD, in order of difficulty, so players can master new techniques, then move on to more challenging material.
00000274 Book/CD Pack $17.95

SCALES AND MODES IN THE BEGINNING
by Ron Middlebrook
The most comprehensive and complete scale book written especially for the guitar. Chapers include: Fretboard Visualization • Scale Terminology • Scales and Modes • and a Scale to Chord Guide.
00000010 ....$11.95

SLIDE GUITAR AND OPEN TUNINGS
by Doug Cox
Explores the basics of open tunings and slide guitar for the intermediate player, including licks, chords, songs and patterns. This is not just a repertoire book, but rather an approach for guitarists to jam with others, invent their own songs, and understand how to find their way around open tunings with and without a slide. The accompanying CD features 37 tracks.
00000243 Book/CD Pack $17.95

SPEED METAL
by Dave Celentano
In an attempt to teach the aspiring rock guitarist how to pick faster and play more melodically, Dave Celentano uses heavy metal neo-classical styles from Paganini and Bach to rock in this great book/CD pack. The book is structured to take the player through the examples in order of difficulty.
00000261 Book/CD Pack $17.95

25 WAYS TO IMPROVE YOUR SOLO GUITAR PLAYING
by Jay Marks
Keep your music fresh with the great ideas in this new book! Covers: chords, dynamics, harmonics, phrasing, intros & endings and more!
00000323 Book/CD Pack $19.95

Centerstream Publishing, LLC
P.O Box 17878 - Anaheim Hills, CA 92817
P/Fax (714)-779-9390 - Email: Centerstream@aol.com
Website: www.centerstream-usa.com